The Kickstarter Handbook

THE KICKSTARTER HANDBOOK

Real-Life Crowdfunding Success Stories

By Don Steinberg

QUIRK BOOKS
PHILADELPHIA

Library of Congress Cataloging in Publication Number: 2012938104

ISBN: 978-1-59474-608-6

Printed in Canada

Typeset in Bembo and ITC Franklin Gothic

Design by Katie Hatz
Production management by John J. McGurk

Quirk Books
215 Church Street
Philadelphia, PA 19106
quirkbooks.com

10 9 8 7 6 5 4 3 2 1

CONTENTS

Introduction: What Is Kickstarter 7
. . . and do people really give you money?

Chapter 1: Are You Ready for This? 19
What you must know before you start to Kickstart

Chapter 2: Choosing Your Magic Number 31
How to pick the right financial target for your Kickstarter campaign

Chapter 3: Pledges and Rewards 51
The calculated art of choosing rewards for your backers

Chapter 4: Who Gives? 71
The backstory on backers

Chapter 5: How Long Will This Be Going On? 85
A brief chapter on duration

Chapter 6: Lights, Camera, Action 91
Making the all-important Kickstarter video

Chapter 7: The Kickoff! 105
Build your project and launch it

Chapter 8: Build the Buzz 119
How to get attention via mass media and social networks

Chapter 9: The Finishing Kick 147
It's time to cross the goal line, plus four frantic finishes

Chapter 10: After the Loving: Tales of Fulfillment 161
Delivering the goods to your generous backers

Chapter 11: Learning from Failure 179
Kickstarter misfires, redemptions, and second acts

Chapter 12: Resources and Kickstarter Alternatives 193
More ways to get it started

Appendix 207
Your Kickstarter Campaign Prelaunch Worksheet

Index 219

Introduction
WHAT IS KICKSTARTER?

. . . and do people really *give you money?*

S COTT THRIFT DREAMED OF DESIGNING a new kind of clock.

Instead of having the usual hour hand and minute hand and second hand relentlessly ticking away, his clock would have just a single white hand that would take a full year to go all the way around, its sweep through time practically imperceptible from moment to moment. Instead of numbers around its circumference, the clock's face would display the full spectrum of color, a gradient from icy blue in winter to verdant green in spring, brilliant yellow in summer and leaf red in the fall.

He was imagining a beautiful piece of wall art. But his vision wasn't really about the clock so much as his outlook on life, which is that if we encounter time only in terms of its hurtling, transient passage, we may fail to appreciate what is happening now, in the present.

"I'm at war with seconds," Thrift says. "The second hand is a recent invention. I think it's only 120 years old or so. It damages the way that life actually is. There's a larger scale at work."

Thrift dreamed that an alternative to time's most overbearing taskmaster, the traditional wall clock, might help. He first had the idea in 2004. He spent years refining his concept, initially working on it in his head and then building a prototype. He imagined it would be great if the annual clock became an object he could make and sell to like-minded people across the planet. But Thrift lacked expertise in manufacturing. He wasn't even a product designer. He's a filmmaker in Brooklyn. Besides, any attempt to produce even a small number of the clocks could be costly—there were unresolved questions about the design and materials, and it would require reinventing the way the gears and electronics worked. A clock that doesn't tell time isn't exactly the sort of thing you can raise money to manufacture; it's not as though a buyer from Walmart would be eager to place an order. We live in a world where ideas are funded based on the amount of revenue they are projected to produce.

So, like a lot of product designers Thrift was encountering by late 2011, he tried Kickstarter, a website where an artist, designer, or inventor can create a page that describes a project, and then anyone anywhere can contribute money to help make the idea a reality. He gave his invention a name that would remind everyone what it celebrated: "The Present." He posted a description of his project on Kickstarter.com. It included a video that mixed quick-cut life-flashing-before-your-eyes imagery with earnest electronic music, showed his design concept for the clock, and asked potential backers: "How can you live in the moment when the moment changes every second?"

"I explained on the Kickstarter page that part of the funding would be to hire a product designer, to rethink everything," he says. "Is this the best way to do it? Should we do it in ceramic? What's the best printing? I was convinced that I had brought the idea as far as I could. I felt confident enough that it was something I could talk about, that I had taken it to the edge."

Through Kickstarter, he asked the world for $24,000 to help him produce the Present. Backers could pledge $2 and receive a rainbow-colored digital image of the clock face as a thank-you. They could pledge $120 to receive one of the clocks, essentially preordering a product that didn't exist yet and might never exist without their help. In thirty days, Thrift raised $97,567 from 867 backers worldwide.

As surprising or unconventional as it sounds, Thrift's tale is typical of what has been happening on Kickstarter since the site formally launched in 2009. More than 20,000 inventors, designers, filmmakers, musicians, authors, painters, game developers, choreographers, poets, and other artists have used the site to raise money for their projects, in many cases for traditional starving-artist reasons.

"I had booked shows for a tour, and I was basically deciding whether I was going to go on a payment plan for my property taxes or ask my parents for money, and that was an option I had used too many times," says Nano Whitman, a folkie musician based in Austin, Texas, who asked for $11,000—and raised $15,950—on Kickstarter in 2011. "It wasn't just the tour. I needed to press my records. I'd booked time in a studio. I had lined up PR for the tour. I made a lot of commitments that were going to cost me money, before I knew how I was going to pay for them. I think, for musicians, that's totally normal. If you waited until you had money before you started lining up projects, you'd never do most of them."

Can something like Kickstarter really exist?

Kickstarter is one of those rare so-crazy-it-just-might-work ideas that did in fact work. Who would've imagined it? A website where a person can present an idea, ask people for money, and *people give it to you*? Really?

Face it: people don't easily part with their cash, even on the Internet. One might say *especially* on the Internet. Most of the Web's biggest successes are popular for one simple reason: they're free. You don't have to pay to use Google, Twitter, Facebook, YouTube, Wikipedia, and thousands of other hugely popular sites. Web users have been spoiled by free searching and free social networks, free online newspapers, free magazines, free videos, free software, free maps, free blogging tools, free e-mail, free video conferencing, free online storage, and free porn. And that's not even counting the wide world of music and movie piracy. The Internet has even redefined the word *sharing* to require less of an out-of-pocket commitment. *Sharing* used to mean that if Annie had three cookies in her lunchbox and she gave one of them to Johnny, she was left with two for herself. Today sharing can be sacrifice free. Just post a link or pass along a copy of a song or a photo, which maybe you never owned in the first place, and it doesn't diminish your own stash one bit.

So amid this pay-nothing-to-play ethos, how does one explain the explosive growth of Kickstarter, where, as of March 2012, Web users had pledged more than $165 million? Kickstarter runs counter to conventional logic in so many ways that it almost defies gravity. It evokes that old Monty Python comedy sketch where a meek fund-raiser approaches a rich businessman, waving a tin can, asking for a donation of one British pound.

"I don't want to seem stupid," the businessman says, "but it looks to me as though I'm a pound down on the whole deal." Yes, the fund-raiser says, that's how it works. And the businessman replies: "Good lord! That's the most exciting new idea I've heard in years! It's so simple, it's brilliant!"

Where it all began

Some might say the idea of Kickstarter itself is so simple, it's brilliant. The person who imagined it is Perry Chen, whose prior adventures had included everything from day-trading to opening an art gallery. As the now-legendary Kickstarter origin story goes, in 2002 Chen was living in New Orleans, unemployed, messing around with electronic music. He wanted to throw a big party featuring the Austrian DJs Kruder and Dorfmeister, but he figured it would cost $15,000 to stage the event and wasn't sure he'd be able to sell enough tickets to cover the expense. That's when the seedling of the Kickstarter idea began to sprout. If only there was a way he could ask people to pledge to buy tickets in advance, to show their support for the DJ party. If advance pledges were enough to cover the costs, then it would be party time!

Chen never followed through on the DJ party but took the advance-funding idea with him when he moved to New York City. There, while waiting tables at a Brooklyn restaurant, he met Yancey Strickler, a music journalist, who agreed that the concept was pretty sweet and potentially a useful website for struggling artists like themselves. They connected with Charles Adler, a user-interface-design expert, who helped with the look of the site. Being liberal-arts guys, they had to hire a techie to write the computer code. In 2008 they launched informally as KickStartr.com, with $200,000 in funding from backers including the comedian David Cross, who knew somebody they knew. Later they bought a vowel and became Kickstarter, formally launching in 2009.

The site had a few basic rules from the get-go. A Kickstarter project had to fall within the creative arts (the founders came up with thirteen categories) and could not be a fund-raising initiative for a charity (see chapter 1 for more on Kickstarter regulations). Another fundamental rule was that creators had to declare the amount they wanted to raise and set a deadline date; if the stated funding target was not reached by the deadline, all pledges would be erased. The creator would get nothing. That made sense in the context of the original DJ-party idea. If Chen had raised only $10,000 of the $15,000 he needed for that party, he'd be committed to staging the event while facing a $5,000 loss before he even started. Why create that possibility? When there's a make-or-break fund-raising target, the pledges become a sort of vote on whether a project has enough support to exist, whether it deserves to be born. The target also becomes its own entity. Many artists and product designers who have run Kickstarter campaigns attest that the target dollar amount evolves into a kind of group destination, and on the Web it acts like a magnet, attracting pledges with its own force. "I think the all-or-nothing formula is part of what makes it work," Strickler said in an interview. "It's part of the game-ification of life. If something is getting close, the Internet comes alive and makes it happen."

Another tenet of the Kickstarter rule book was that pledging money to a project created neither debt nor equity. That is, money given through the Kickstarter site isn't a loan and never needs to be repaid. And it isn't an opportunity to buy a share of a fledgling company as a way to receive a share of profits later. It's simply: *here's some money.* Backers often do feel invested in the Kickstarter project they supported because they were there at its inception, but they aren't literally invested in it. They may feel a sense of ownership, helping to birth an idea before the world knew about it, but they don't have any legal ownership.

The earliest Kickstarter campaigns, to test the waters, proved that the site was functional. In one primitive project titled "drawing for dollars" (note that we're talking about the primordial days of May 2009), a cartoon illustrator sought to raise $20 to custom-draw a picture. He got $35. The site grew fast, evolving from a home for offbeat art ideas to a place where serious designers could test the viability of their products. In November 2010, a project to create a tripod mount for the iPhone, called Glif, attracted 5,273 backers and raised $137,417. In December 2010, the TikTok and LunaTik wristbands, which would allow a user to wear an iPod nano music player as a wristwatch, raised close to $1 million from 13,512 backers. Born as a so-crazy-it-just-might-work notion, Kickstarter was quickly becoming a breeding ground to nurture more such outlandish ideas.

But even then, Kickstarter had barely shifted into second gear.

By 2011, *Publishers Weekly* magazine calculated that Kickstarter had become the No. 3 publisher of indie graphic novels in the United States, in terms of the number of book projects it funded. The 2012 Sundance Film Festival, a major showcase for independent films, featured seventeen movies that had received Kickstarter funding, amounting to 10 percent of the festival's lineup. Early in 2012, Kickstarter announced that it expected to fund creative projects to the tune of $150 million for the year, a slightly larger sum than the 2012 fiscal year budget for the National Endowment for the Arts. (Kickstarter keeps 5 percent of all project funding, so the company and its early backers are clearly doing fine financially.)

Along the way, a new word was born for a novel way to support arts and invention: *crowdfunding*. It's yet another way that the reach of the Internet has been put to work. Thousands of individuals contributed information to help build the free online encyclopedia Wikipedia—that's *crowdsourcing*. Turn that into money, and you have crowdfunding, a means of moving money among people, circumventing traditional sources and decision makers and gatekeepers, a sort of grassroots redistribution of wealth. Kickstarter is part of a diverse ecosystem offering new ways for people to connect with one another online, to exchange ideas, stuff, and sometimes hard currency. That universe broadly includes eBay and other auction sites, where buyers and sellers find each other and one person's extra money is swapped for another person's vintage vinyl LPs. It includes Kiva, a microlending site where you can loan $25 to a pig farmer in Senegal or a seamstress in Guatemala. It includes Team Continuum, where you can volunteer to run in a marathon to raise money for a cancer patient. It's all about sharing wealth and ideas and work in ways that weren't so easy before the Web.

The folks at Kickstarter like to point out that this shiny new business model for artists and entrepreneurs is in fact a sort of throwback to much earlier times. Painters have long depended on patrons to put up money in advance. Classical composers, such as Mozart and Beethoven, sometimes relied on "subscriptions" similar to Kickstarter's system, allowing them to advertise for pledges to finance concerts or printed editions of their work.

For product development, too, crowdfunding creates markets for products that otherwise might never be born. "The most amazing thing is that the product doesn't exist, but they're making it exist through their funding. It's not like I had clocks on the shelf," says Scott Thrift. "The way the market has been driven throughout history is there's some company that puts out a product and expects you to buy it. This is totally different. It's a collaborative process. It's a beautiful thing. Kickstarter is just one of the most brilliant ideas I think I've seen on the Web since Google. It's such a strong use of what the Web really is."

Adds Josh Hartung, who raised $34,123 in December 2011 to produce a paper-lamp-making kit called Loomi: "I think some of the magic is that you can create these small companies around products that would normally not be feasible to bring to the mass market. Through Kickstarter, you can reach these niches. I just funded a project for a collapsible sunglasses case. It's ingenious. You can bring out these products that would never be able to come out if left up to, say, Sony."

Because Kickstarter has become so popular, it can bring attention to artists and entrepreneurs that goes beyond the art or the products they offer on the site. "I had no idea the response would be so big," says Joshua Harker, a sculptor in Chicago who raised $77,271 to create cool-looking plastic skulls using 3-D printing technology. "Not only have hundreds of thousands of people been exposed to my work, but I have a thousand new collectors who didn't exist for me previously. That is huge. I have had job, project, collaboration, movie, exhibition, and lecture offers. This is the type of game changer I had been working for, and something the gallery/exhibition circuit has not been able to provide. Kickstarter put me in front of everyone that matters to me in forty-five days."

Now it's your turn

I know what you're thinking. You're thinking you might like a piece of this action. You have a great idea, too, after all. Your dream to create a radio show featuring the world's best ventriloquists and their dummies has been building inside you like an ache, crying for release. You just know that your product could revolutionize the world of dog grooming, or pencil sharpening, or both, if only you had enough money to make it real. Or maybe you'd simply like to join the Kickstarter gold rush while the prospecting is hot, gather ideas to figure out what sort of project might be successful and how to do it right. All that is what this book is for.

No one says the task will be easy. Chapter 1 is meant, in part, to scare you and prepare you for the massive amount of work that a successful Kickstarter campaign can demand. Everything in this book is based on research into real Kickstarter projects. Dozens of people connected with Kickstarter campaigns have been generous enough to share the biggest and the smallest details of their efforts. What worked and what didn't. What challenges, surprises, and failures they confronted. How they decided they were ready for Kickstarter, settled on their fund-raising goals and their rewards and pledge amounts, made their videos, attracted attention through the media and social networks, and fulfilled their promises to backers by shipping goods after their projects were successful. The book also includes financial worksheets and helpful lists and charts. Some names will recur throughout the chapters, and you'll become familiar with their projects. Sometimes we just let them talk. They're the ones who have lived through the process, and their experiences are the best textbook.

We also use distinctive terminology that has become standard on not been able to provide. Kickstarter put me in front of everyone that matters to me in forty-five days."

Now it's your turn

I know what you're thinking. You're thinking you might like a piece of this action. You have a great idea, too, after all. Your dream to create a radio show featuring the world's best ventriloquists and their dummies has been building inside you like an ache, crying for release. You just know that your product could revolutionize the world of dog grooming, or pencil sharpening, or both, if only you had enough money to make it real. Or maybe you'd simply like to join the Kickstarter gold rush while the prospecting is hot, gather ideas to figure out what sort of project might be successful and how to do it right. All that is what this book is for.

No one says the task will be easy. Chapter 1 is meant, in part, to scare you and prepare you for the massive amount of work that a successful Kickstarter campaign can demand. Everything in this book is based on research into real Kickstarter projects. Dozens of people connected with Kickstarter campaigns have been generous enough to share the biggest and the smallest details of their efforts. What worked and what didn't. What challenges, surprises, and failures they confronted. How they decided they were ready for Kickstarter, settled on their fund-raising goals and their rewards and pledge amounts, made their videos, attracted attention through the media and social networks, and fulfilled their promises to backers by shipping goods after their projects were successful. The book also includes financial worksheets and helpful lists and charts. Some names will recur throughout the chapters, and you'll become familiar with their projects. Sometimes we just let them talk. They're the ones who have lived through the process, and their experiences are the best textbook.

We also use distinctive terminology that has become standard on

Kickstarter. For example, by posting a creative project on Kickstarter to raise funding, and setting it up to run for a certain number of days, you are starting a "campaign." Someone who launches a Kickstarter campaign may be referred to as a "creator." People who donate money are called "backers," and what they give is a "pledge." When a project reaches its financial target, it is considered "funded." The items that backers receive as thanks for their pledges are always called "rewards."

People who are hip about all things Kickstarter occasionally refer to a campaign as, simply, "a Kickstarter." A person who launches a campaign may also be called "a Kickstarter." So, yeah, a Kickstarter can launch a Kickstarter on Kickstarter. Hey, it's a flexible word, and the author and publisher of this book don't have to pay a royalty every time we use it, so there you go. Most of the rest of the stuff that happens on Kickstarter can be described using normal, everyday English, and we don't anticipate any confusion.

So what are you waiting for? Let's get this dance party started. As one Kickstarter campaign creator might say: there's no time like the Present.

1.

ARE YOU READY
FOR THIS?

What you must know before you start to Kickstart

IT'S EASY TO HEAR THE TALES of Kickstarter hauls so gargantuan that your eyes light up like silver dollars while the cash-register sound from Pink Floyd's song "Money" plays in your head. Did two Brooklyn product designers really rake in $281,989 to make stainless-steel pen holders, after asking for just $2,500? Yes, they did. Did a crew of civic-minded movie buffs seriously receive $67,436 in pledges to erect a statue of RoboCop in downtown Detroit? Yup. Did an illustrator in Philadelphia rake in $1.25 million to print books of his Web comics? Indeed. All those things really happened, and more.

The numbers are alluring—and may be deceiving. They might lead you to imagine Kickstarter as a magical candyland of tangerine streams and marmalade skies (and, most of all, pennies from heaven) where benefactors are milling around with oozing checkbooks, just waiting for you to show up so they can click Donate and lavish their munificence upon you. *This is gonna be easy money*, you think.

Think again.

You don't hit the jackpot on Kickstarter just by pulling the lever. Yes, a portion of the funding in pretty much every successful campaign does come from benevolent strangers or remote acquaintances who kick in money because either they think your project is awesome and worthy or they just want a chunk of the soap you're selling. But even mysterious benefactors need to find out about the project. And it's still real money. Potential backers need to be sold on the concept and your ability to execute it. And so do the people you thought you could rely on unfailingly (i.e., your parents and siblings and so-called "friends").

For the month or so that your Kickstarter campaign lasts, it can be a relentless, all-consuming effort, one in which you are required to ask loved ones and casual acquaintances and total strangers for money, begging desperately for donations, and then maybe begging some more. You'll grovel for attention from journalists and bloggers. You'll pray to the online gods that a sympathetic Web editor who works at Kickstarter will highlight your project as a "Staff Pick" or, dare to dream, "Project of the Day." All that while your personal goal is festering out there in public, submitted for approval, or rejection, by the entire world.

And that's *before* you even undertake the work of making your awesome moose-themed mural, or USB-controlled pancake griddle, or nu metal folk album, or whatever it is that your project promises that you'll do.

The process is not for the timid or fainthearted. Felix Dennis, the international publishing mogul and self-made multimillionaire who titled his amusing memoir *How to Get Rich*, writes about the fortitude you must bring to any effort that involves asking others for money so that you can get started (as he did). Although he's talking about getting filthy rich, not launching a Kickstarter campaign, the same principles apply: "If you are not prepared to work longer hours than almost anyone you know, despite the jibes of colleagues and friends, you are unlikely to get rich," he writes. "If you care what the neighbors think, you will never get rich. . . . The truth is that getting rich means sacrifice. And the worst of it is, it isn't always *you* that's doing the sacrificing." In those hard nuggets of advice, just swap out "get rich" and insert "successfully fund a Kickstarter campaign."

It's more than an adventure; it's a job

"One of the things we learned is—it's a job. It's not free money," says Brandon Walley, one of the principals of the project called **Detroit Needs A Statue of Robocop!** "A couple of us were here in Detroit . . . and it was like a full-time job for a while. Making sure you get the word out, constant social media stuff." Pete Taylor agrees. "It's unreal," Taylor said, two days into his campaign to raise $12,000 to launch **SAVORx**, a service to provide fresh spices and spicy recipes to foodies. "I haven't slept in two days."

"We weren't very smart about it. I think we kind of assumed if we put it on Kickstarter people would magically flock to the project," Dave Chenell told the Betabeat blog, after he and friend Eric Cleckner raised only $3,049 of their $20,000 goal to make **graFighters**, "an online fighting game for your hand-drawn characters."

Aurora Guerrero, a filmmaker in Los Angeles, set out to raise $80,000 to finish *Mosquita y Mari*, a feature-length film about a relationship between two Latina teenagers. "I've told people, if you're going to launch a campaign where you're trying to raise more than $10,000, then you'd better get ready to work," she says. "Work your butt off. Even before you do the campaign. You need to do research. What are your incentives? What's your goal gonna be? Create a team to help you, because you can't do it by yourself. If you try to do it on your own, your life's going to be miserable for thirty days or however long. We had somebody doing online social media every day during the campaign for thirty days straight."

Says Bill Lichtenstein, a veteran filmmaker and fund-raiser who sought to raise $104,000 to make **The American Revolution**, a documentary about Boston rock-radio station WBCN: "If you look at almost any account of anybody who's done one of these things, usually they'll say, 'don't do more than thirty days. It will kill you. Or plan to take a two-week vacation afterward. It's exhausting.' I thought, how exhausting can it be? It's like eBay! But it's not."

"The Kickstarter thing is so dramatically divergent from anything I've done. I mean, I've been fund-raising now for fifteen years, and it's unlike anything, drawing much more from my experience on Election Day or community organizing. People who think 'Oh, I'll just put something up and raise $10,000' are horribly disappointed. Part of it is that if you don't raise all of it, you get nothing. That's why it's like Election Day. You have one shot. So every minute you're thinking about it, handing out cards. You're talking to a cabdriver and you go, 'Hey, here's a film I'm pitching.'"

A clinical way to look at Kickstarter is to view it as merely a billboard and an accounting system—a central place to tell the world what you're offering, along with a mechanism for collecting and tallying donations. The rest is up to you, and the work you'll need to do and the connections you'll need to pursue are not that different from what you'd have to do in a world without Kickstarter.

But to those who have achieved their fund-raising targets, Kickstarter does seem like more than just a tool. "There is some magic in it that I will never be able to put words to," says Guerrero. "I felt like it was the universe saying: it's time. After Kickstarter, we were at full speed. We wrapped the film—we went into preproduction for June and shot in July. We got a postproduction grant and were in post through October before we submitted to Sundance."

Lichtenstein thinks that although Kickstarter may not exactly be a honey pot dripping with sweet, free cash, neither is it like cold-calling unsympathetic people who have no idea what you're talking about. "I think it's somewhere in the middle," he says. Anyone who comes to your Kickstarter page is likely to be aware of the basic idea of it, open to the notion that a creative project is seeking support, maybe willing to try a new experience. "It's kind of like Club Med, a place where all these single people are looking to hook up and meet other people. It's not like walking up to a stranger and saying, *Hey, wanna come home with me?*"

Clearing the low hurdles

Your first gauntlet of requirements before you begin a Kickstarter campaign is easy enough to ace. It's sort of like the horizontal line drawn about four feet high on signs at the entrances to the scarier amusement park rides. You have to be *this tall* to ride. For Kickstarter:

* You must be at least 18 years old.
* You must be a U.S. resident with a Social Security Number (or EIN).
* You must have a U.S. address, a U.S. bank account, and U.S. state-issued ID (driver's license).
* You must have a major U.S. credit or debit card.
* You will have to establish an Amazon Payments account and link it to your bank account.

Basically, you need to be an adult in America with the usual stuff. But, hey, enough about you. Next come two key questions about the nature of your project. Aside from screening for prohibited content, these two questions constitute the only official criteria that the Kickstarter staff uses to decide whether you may proceed with launching a campaign. The only things they need are "yes" answers to:

1. Does it serve a creative purpose?

2. Is it a project?

Both of these questions need to be explained a little more. They are in fact a little squishy and potentially generous with wiggle room.

But first, here is the official list of prohibited subject matter that will get your project rejected from Kickstarter before it ever starts:

Prohibited Subject Matter on Kickstarter

* Items not directly produced by the project or its creator (you can't offer things from the garage, repackaged existing products, weekends at the resort, etc.)
* Alcohol (prohibited as a reward)
* Contests (entry fees, prize money, within your project to encourage support, etc)
* Cosmetics
* Coupons, discounts, and cash-value gift cards
* Drugs, druglike substances, drug paraphernalia, tobacco, etc.
* Electronic surveillance equipment
* Energy drinks
* Financial incentives (ownership, share of profits, repayment/loans, etc.)
* Firearms, weapons, and knives
* Health, medical, and safety-related products
* Multilevel marketing and pyramid programs
* Nutritional supplements
* Offensive material (hate speech, inappropriate content, etc.)
* Projects endorsing or opposing a political candidate
* Pornographic material
* Promoting or glorifying acts of violence
* Raffles, lotteries, and sweepstakes
* Real estate
* Self-help books, DVDs, CDs, etc.

source: Kickstarter

Does it serve a creative purpose?

Kickstarter was founded by artists with the idea of helping creative work come to life. As much as you'd like to help your friend Agatha pay for her bunion surgery by holding an online fund-raiser, Kickstarter is not the place to do it. It isn't for charities. Prohibited uses, according to the site's guidelines, include "raising money for the Red Cross, funding an awareness campaign, funding a scholarship, or donating a portion of funds raised on Kickstarter to a charity or cause." There are crowdfunding sites online for charitable causes, such as Crowdrise.com (see chapter 12 for more of these types of websites). A Kickstarter campaign also can't be for a "fund my life" project: to pay tuition or bills, to go on vacation, or even to buy art supplies without a specific purpose and project in mind.

"Creative purpose" means that it needs to be classifiable into one of Kickstarter's thirteen creative categories: Art, Comics, Dance, Design, Fashion, Film, Food, Games, Music, Photography, Publishing, Technology, and Theater. The gatekeepers at Kickstarter headquarters profess to make no aesthetic judgments about your project. They don't care if you're cool or you're square. They don't judge whether a project is right for Kickstarter's image. They're not grading your movie's plot structure. They're not asking how much experience your drummer has.

Is it a "project"?

The other requirement is that your project needs to have a discrete goal, a clearly articulated objective. That is, if you get the money you asked for, you will produce a particular thing—an album, a film, a machine, a book, a new way to keep the surface of beverage bottles from getting moist on muggy days, and the like. Kickstarter is not supposed to be used for ongoing expenses for a business or as a general way of obtaining seed money for a start-up company. It gets a little squishy, though. Plenty of companies have been born because

Kickstarter funding helped them produce their first gadget, or game, or clock, or smooth stones that control the temperature of your cup of coffee (this last was a real Kickstarter, called **Coffee Joulies**).

"The idea of a creative project is a made-up one. It's kind of a fuzzy line," Kickstarter cofounder Yancey Strickler has acknowledged. The brass at Kickstarter feels that even if what you're really doing is starting a company, and the product in your campaign is its genesis, Kickstarter wants the campaign to be about the product, not the company. By the same token, if you want to assemble a ska band to make an album, the album is the project. If you promise the album to backers and deliver it, Kickstarter considers its purpose served. The long-term survival of the band isn't the goal.

An ideal Kickstarter project also benefits backers as much as the creator. The way the Kickstarter team sees it, it should be about personal achievement rather than commercial interest. Or at least you're well advised to present it that way. You want to be saying: "We have this awesome idea—help us make it a reality!" Not: "We have this profitable idea—help us commercialize it!"

Are you ready for your close-up?

OK, so you're ready to rock. You're pretty sure you're psychologically prepared to launch a Kickstarter campaign. You've blocked out the time to make it work. Your project appears to qualify as legitimate for posting on the site. The only remaining question is: is your project ready for prime time?

Although funny to say, the name Kickstarter is a bit of a misnomer. Many of the most successful Kickstarter projects have not started from scratch at all. Many were in development for months or even years before arriving on the site, having been developed by creators who had long before then built reputations and developed devoted fan bases. Tim Schafer, who smashed Kickstarter fund-raising records in March 2012 when he attracted $3.3 million in pledges for the **Double Fine Adventure** video game, was a known game developer who'd spent more than a decade at LucasArts creating such industry hits as Grim Fandango, Monkey Island, and Psychonauts. Scott Wilson, who in late 2010 raised $942,578 for the **TikTok** and **LunaTik** wristbands, which turn an iPod nano into a wristwatch, is a former creative director for Nike whose work has been displayed in museums. **The Order of the Stick Reprint Drive**, which in early 2012 drew $1.25 million in pledges for Philadelphia illustrator Rich Burlew, was set up to print books of Burlew's existing webcomics; the passionate fan base he'd spent years developing drove his funding total to dizzying new heights every day.

Many filmmakers bringing projects to Kickstarter are not pitching dreamy notions that exist only on paper; rather, they are seeking funding either to wrap up filming or for postproduction. They may have plenty of footage in the can, ready to show potential backers. Musicians who take to Kickstarter to make an album likely have songs written, with many or all of them recorded, and they're looking for money to engineer and produce a CD. If you have a product idea, it's highly advisable to have progressed beyond the idea phase before you even venture onto the Kickstarter platform. "Definitely have a functional prototype if possible. Otherwise people don't really believe that you can deliver," says Peter Seid, a cocreator of **Romo – the Smartphone Robot**, which drew $114,796 in pledges in late 2011. In fact, Kickstarter has been tightening its guidelines specifically for product design projects, asking would-be creators to provide detailed information about their background and experience, plus a manufacturing plan (for hardware projects) and a working prototype.

In a way, Kickfinisher might be as apt a name for the site. After all, it's about carrying an undone project to completion. Of course, it's all part of an ongoing process. You're wrapping up one project to make your next creative steps possible. Like that grand old cliché they dust off when you graduate from high school: they call it commencement because it isn't an ending; it's a beginning.

Kickstarter has funded thousands of creative projects, and there's no reason you can't join that club. If this chapter has been a little scary, cautionary, even discouraging, that's intentional. You want to be completely ready to roll when that curtain opens and the audience quiets to examine you. If you're going to ask your friends for their money and time, you need it to be for something you're truly passionate about and a hundred percent committed to. If that is indeed the case, if you've got your act together, if your project is ready to present to the public, if you need the money enough to work for it, then you are ready to go for it on Kickstarter.

The next steps, and the next chapters, will carry you into the fray. Here's what you'll need to do next:

→ decide what your project is and how you want to tell your story

→ decide how much money you need to raise to make it happen

→ decide what rewards you will give to backers, and attach specific pledge dollar amounts to specific rewards

→ decide on a duration for your Kickstarter campaign, setting a fund-raising deadline

→ make a video explaining and promoting your project

→ know in advance who are your likely backers and outlets for media publicity, and be prepared to contact them

→ set up your campaign page on the Kickstarter website and launch it

2.

CHOOSING YOUR
MAGIC NUMBER

How to pick the right financial target for your
Kickstarter campaign

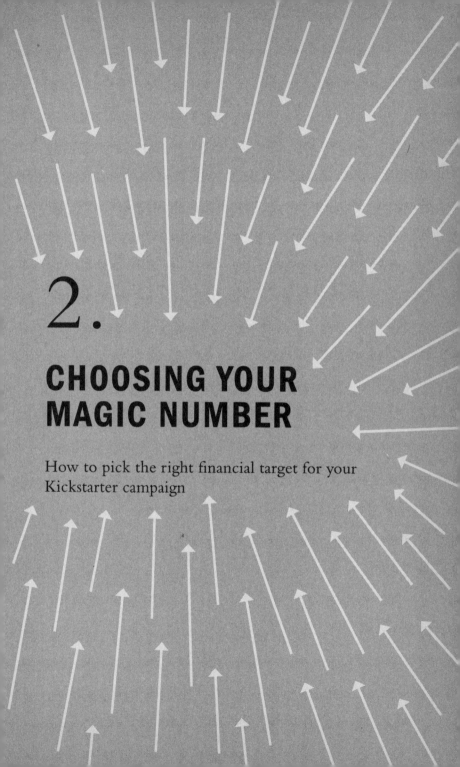

I N OCTOBER 2011, three brash young advertising professionals
launched a Kickstarter campaign to raise $3.5 million. They said
they wanted to buy time during the NFL Super Bowl telecast
to air a "kick-ass" commercial that would celebrate the state
of Kentucky. They made a funny two-minute video during which,
sitting in front of a life-sized cutout of Colonel Sanders, they extolled
the Bluegrass State's virtues and famous natives and some other
goofball stuff. Amazingly, people pledged more than $112,000 to their
Kickstarter campaign. Crazy, right? But forget about it: it was funny
money. Backers knew they'd never have to pay up, because spending
$3.5 million for a joke was pretty much ... a joke. The campaign failed
as anything but a publicity stunt.

Kickstarter uses an all-or-nothing funding model called the
threshold pledge system. You establish a target monetary amount,
and if you fail to reach that goal by the deadline you set, you receive
nada. Any amount anyone has pledged is erased. "It's like Cinderella
at midnight. It just goes away," says one filmmaker.

Because of this all-or-nothing system, determining the amount you
should set as your Kickstarter fund-raising goal is itself an art, a mix
between hardcore financial calculation and game of chance. Do you
go for every penny you think you can squeeze out of people? Or ask
for just enough to cover your costs? If you're more serious than those

lucky-in-Kentucky boys, it's crucial to set a realistic, attainable fund-raising goal. Your instinct might be to set a low goal, just to be safe. But beware: you don't want to sell your idea short by raising too little to pull it off. In fact, it may be better to aim high and fall short, and therefore not be obligated to do anything, rather than to underestimate the cost of your project, attain a fund-raising target that is too low, and find yourself holding the bag to complete a project with an inadequate budget.

There's no one-size-fits-all answer to the above scenarios, but here is a pretty good golden rule: **you need to raise enough money to cover the cost of your project, plus the cost of fulfilling the rewards you've promised to backers**. And there's one added consideration: **your total pledge target needs to cover your costs after you subtract Kickstarter and Amazon Payments fees**. From whatever amount you raise, Kickstarter takes a 5 percent fee of the amount you raise, and Amazon Payments takes 3 to 5 percent, too, depending on some complicated calculations involving backers' credit card processing.

The way these amounts can add up is interesting (and this chapter contains two sample financial worksheets to show this). For example, if you need $25,000 to produce a film, you may need to raise closer to $35,000 in Kickstarter pledges. That extra $10,000 would cover about $6,000 in reward-fulfillment costs (sending out promised DVDs and such to your backers) and around $3,000 in fees to Kickstarter and Amazon, in addition to other expenses related to running the campaign.

To guide you in setting up a fund-raising goal for your Kickstarter campaign, we've provided a few pieces of essential information. First, we have two different financial worksheets. They're simplified customized-for-Kickstarter versions of what an accountant might call a profit-and-loss statement. After these, and for a more organic take on the subject, we include interviews with multiple successful Kickstarter campaign creators, in which they explain how they set their fund-raising targets and what factors they considered.

Doing the math: Two Kickstarter campaign cost/revenue worksheets

The science of setting a Kickstarter fund-raising target is inexact. It's a crazy calculus that involves forecasting your costs and receipts without knowing how many pledges you'll get or how many rewards you'll need to provide. It differs depending on the type of project. If your aim is to create leather Kindle Fire cases that double as bicycle seats, or any other gadget or invention, you will essentially be preselling the items by offering to produce and send them to backers who pledge a certain dollar amount. Your expenses will vary widely depending on how many backers pledge at the level required to obtain a finished product. In that case, your aim may be to give birth to an ongoing business based on that product, so you may also want to have excess inventory after the Kickstarter campaign is complete.

On the other hand, if your Kickstarter is aimed at funding a one-time creative endeavor, such as a film or an album, a stage performance or a work of art, your campaign-related finances will be different. For example, for a film with a budget of $25,000, you mainly have one large fixed cost that won't change based on the number of pledges (though if you promise to mail out DVDs to backers, you will have to factor in some variable costs and variable revenues).

Individuals from the artsy side of the aisle may feel a little outgunned by this business-school forecasting. Fear not. We've got these two financial worksheets to help you understand and figure out the kind of reward price/cost structure you need to meet your funding goal (or, conversely, what goal seems realistic based on how many pledges you think you'll get).

This may seem to be jumping into the deep end with some very specific information about your project that you don't have yet. But don't worry. You don't have to fill out any worksheets until you're ready, and you can skip ahead for now if you'd like.

Worksheet #1 is best suited for a one-time performance/arts piece for which you want to raise a chunk of money for a single project or event, and you offer rewards like DVDs or T-shirts to entice pledges (we'll have *a lot* more about choosing great rewards in the next chapter and beyond, so don't panic). Worksheet #2 is more suited to a situation in which you have a product design that you want to bring into the world, and you'd like to create a business around that product that might continue beyond its lifespan on Kickstarter. In this case, the product itself is the reward that you send to backers, and you'll want to receive enough pledge money that you can build up some post-Kickstarter inventory to sell to the public.

Both of these worksheets are merely templates, allowing you to input your own numbers and see what kind of pledge amounts and pledge volumes—and rewards costs—will lead to what sorts of results. Feel free to borrow ideas from either sheet or combine them to suit your project.

Worksheet #1

This worksheet is designed for projects where you are trying to fund a single artistic production—a film, an album, an art installation, a stage show. If your project involves manufacturing products—and then sending those products to backers as rewards—you'll want to use Worksheet #2 on page 42.

Kickstarter Financial Worksheet #1

FIXED COSTS FOR PROJECT

main project (film, album, etc.)	$25,000
website expenses	$750
other	$300
TOTAL FIXED COSTS	$26,050

PLEDGES & REWARDS	pledge amount	estimated #	cost per reward	shipping/ reward	pledge revenue	rewards cost	net
REWARD #1: digital content e-mailed to backer							
standard	$10	300	$0	$0	$3,000	$0	$3,000
bulk order	$10	0	$0	$0	$0	$0	$0
international	$10	0	$0	$0	$0	$0	$0
reward count		300					
REWARD #2: small item by mail (DVD, poster)							
standard	$50	200	$5	$3	$10,000	$1,590	$8,410
bulk order	$50	150	$4	$3	$7,500	$1,043	$6,458
international	$66	20	$4	$7	$1,320	$219	$1,101
reward count		370					
REWARD #3: customized version of reward #2							
standard	$80	100	$12	$3	$8,000	$1,500	$6,500
bulk order	$80	0	$12	$3	$0	$0	$0
international	$96	10	$12	$7	$960	$190	$770
reward count		110					
REWARD #4: personalized service with local travel							
standard	$300	15	$100	$0	$4,500	$1,500	$3,000
bulk order	$0	0	$0	$0	$0	$0	$0
international	$0	0	$0	$0	$0	$0	$0
reward count		15					

TOTAL PLEDGES	$35,280
Kickstarter fee (5%)	($1,764)
Amazon Payments fee (3–5%)	($1,411)
TOTAL REWARDS COSTS	$6,042

BOTTOM LINE	YOU GET	COSTS	EXCESS
	$32,105	$32,092	$13

OK, that's a lot of numbers. The gray areas in the worksheet are numbers you don't enter—they are calculations based on the numbers you do enter, those in the white areas. (The green areas—or darker gray for those reading in grayscale—are also calculated numbers, but they're more nice-to-know stats than essential to this worksheet's purpose.) The goal on this worksheet is **to have your total Kickstarter pledge revenues come out equal to or higher than your costs.** That's the bottom line (literally, it's on the worksheet's bottom line).

Here is the information you need to enter into this worksheet, and what it does with your numbers:

Fixed costs: The top of the worksheet is where you enter the anticipated fixed costs for your Kickstarter campaign. It starts with the amount you want to spend to make your film/finish recording your album/erect your statue/stage a choreographed dance production featuring municipal garbage trucks (yes, that is a real Kickstarter project). If you're asking people for money so that you can execute a big project, you need a solid idea of what it's going to cost you. You need to research those expenses. That's the first number on the worksheet.

Your campaign is likely to have other fixed costs that will need to be included in this worksheet's top section. For example, you should add the expenses associated with making your Kickstarter video as a fixed cost of the campaign. If you set up a website for the Kickstarter campaign, that's another fixed cost independent of the number of people who pledge. Web costs can vary widely depending on how ambitious you are. Your site may be simple enough that your only Web-related costs will be for the domain name and site hosting, with you loading all the content yourself. But if you want to set up an online store, that's another level of cost (in our worksheet, it's given as $750). If you need to buy equipment to make your product or your ancillary rewards (for example, a burner to copy DVDs of your film), the cost of that equipment may not vary based on the number of items you need to produce, making it a fixed cost. If you promise to throw a party for all backers who pledge a certain amount, that party will have certain fixed costs associated with it (such as the venue rental) that may not depend on the number of attendees. So, as you can see, you may need to add lines to the fixed-cost section.

Pledge revenue and rewards cost: Here is where you indicate what rewards you've promised to give backers at each pledge level and how much it will cost you to fulfill those promises. In this worksheet we have included four rewards, and each one illustrates a different way the costs may break down. You can add or subtract rewards to suit yourself; they're all set up the same way.

For each reward there are three lines, representing different cost scenarios. To understand these, let's look at Reward #2, which might be a DVD of your film that you promise to ship to backers. The "basic" line in the first column has the basic cost of the pledge, $50. Next is an estimate of how many you think you will "sell." Then come the costs to produce the item and to ship the item to your backer. Obviously, you'll need to research all of these expenses, too.

The second line, labeled "bulk order," takes into account economies of scale or volume discounts that you might receive if you're able to make or order in bulk. In the Reward #2 example, the first 200 DVDs cost $5 each to make and $3 to ship. But the next 150 DVDs cost only $4 apiece to make and the same $3 each to ship. (This is just an example of a volume discount; your numbers will differ.) If you will score progressively better discounts at higher production volumes, add more "bulk order" lines, listing those per-item costs. The third line in each rewards section is for international pledges, for which the shipping expenses will be higher, perhaps substantially so. To protect yourself from having to cover these elevated mailing charges, you may choose to set the pledge level slightly higher for backers who live outside your home country.

Looking back at Reward #1, which lists digital delivery of your content, notice there is no per-item cost or shipping expense. After your fixed expense of setting up a website or online storage account, there's essentially no cost to let people download from the site, even for those living in other countries. That makes this reward highly "profitable," though at $10 it isn't likely to push your total revenue into the stratosphere.

For Reward #3, a customized version of Reward #2—a special color or configuration—there's a higher per-unit production cost and no bulk discount available to you, but the shipping rate is the same as for Reward #2.

For Reward #4, which includes local travel to provide a personal service—say, cooking a meal for people or choreographing a wedding—the cost of travel per reward could fill the cost column, if you can calculate that expense. However, if you'll be renting a truck to use for all your visits, you might list it as a fixed cost instead.

Now for the totals. The "Pledge Revenue" column, in the gray area on the right side of the worksheet, calculates the revenue for every reward scenario by multiplying the pledge amount by the total number of pledges. The "Rewards Cost" column combines the item's manufacturing and shipping costs per reward and multiplies that number by the total number of rewards. (The dark gray-green Net column shows your net gain for each pledge/reward level, so that you can see where most of your "profits" are coming from.)

These Revenue and Cost columns add up to two extremely useful numbers. Total Pledge Revenue is just that: it's all the pledges added together. **That's your Kickstarter number!** (It's $35,280 in our worksheet example.) If all the numbers you put in those white spaces are accurate forecasts, then this number is the amount you would receive in pledges. **That's the figure you should set as your fund-raising goal.**

As noted earlier, your total pledge haul isn't exactly what you will receive to spend on your creative pursuit. First we subtract the 5 percent that Kickstarter receives from each pledge for providing its crowdfunding platform and making your campaign possible. We also subtract the Amazon Payments fee, which as noted earlier is 3 to 5 percent and basically covers the cost of processing backers' credit cards (we've used 4 percent in this model). In this sample worksheet, those deductions turn $35,280 in pledges into $32,105 that goes into your pocket.

Now come the costs to subtract: the fixed costs and the rewards costs added together. For your successful Kickstarter campaign to be truly successful, this sum of all costs needs to be less than or equal to the amount you take in. Here, costs total $32,092, which is less than the amount you'll have received. You did it! And there's even $13 left over for, well, a celebratory pizza.

If it doesn't work out, you can tweak the numbers to see what it would take to make it work. Can you lower your fixed costs? Should you raise a pledge price? Is it realistic to bump up the estimated number of pledges in a given category? Can you add a reward category? Should you reset with lower expectations for everything?

Worksheet #2 (product-oriented campaign)

This worksheet is designed for those campaigns meant to launch a business around a product. It was created by Josh Hartung, a Brooklyn-based mechanical engineer, who was kind enough to allow us to reproduce it here. Hartung was a partner in the successful December 2011 Kickstarter campaign to create and sell **Loomi**, a kit for constructing elegant lamps from thirty-three pieces of die-cut paper. After that campaign, he started the website MakerCapitalist.com to share his ideas about Kickstarter and the make-it-yourself revolution. This sheet doesn't break out different rewards—the lone reward is the product that is the focus of the Kickstarter campaign. In this example, the product costs $20 to make, and it retails for $80. Adding

Kickstarter Expected Results

DESCRIPTION	VALUE	
Retail price	$80	
Number of sales	1200	
% of sales international	30%	
Domestic shipping allowance	$10	
International shipping allowance	$15	
TOTAL EXPECTED KICKSTARTER REVENUE	$113,400	

Kickstarter Direct Costs

DESCRIPTION	TOTAL COST	UNIT COST
Kickstarter & Amazon Pmts	$11,340	
Cost of goods sold	$24,000	$20
Domestic shipping	$9,600	$8
International shipping	$9,000	$25
Fulfillment	$2,400	$2

Business Costs

	TOTAL COST	QUANTITY
Reorder of product for store	$20,000	1000
Website build	$5,000	
Prototyping	$3,000	
Assistants	$2,000	
Marketing and ads	$1,000	
Travel	$1,000	
Contingency	$5,000	
TOTAL PROFIT	$20,060	
Recommended single-unit pledge level	$90	

in shipping costs, it is being made available on Kickstarter for a $90 pledge to domestic backers ($80 plus $10 for shipping) and $95 to international backers ($80 plus $15 for shipping).

This scenario forecasts that 1,200 pledges will come in to generate revenue of $113,400. From that total are subtracted various costs, designed to establish an ongoing business around the product. Notably, it takes out $20,000 to order an additional 1,000 units of the product, inventory to be sold later. After some high start-up costs, including $5,000 for a website that can process orders, $3,000 for prototyping, and $2,000 for assistants, this model also includes a profit of $20,060 to be used toward the future of the business.

Hartung says he crafted this worksheet after completing his real-life **Loomi** campaign. That campaign set out to raise $9,000. "The original goal was based on the bare minimum to make the project go, to meet all the minimums that were required from our tooling people and to hit that first little sweet spot of mass-manufacturing volumes," he explains. The Loomi campaign ended up generating $34,123 in pledges, with 649 backers ordering about 1,000 Loomi kits. It didn't leave much profit, the way the worksheet model here does. But it generated enough pledge revenue to let Hartung and Loomi cocampaigner David Sosnow fulfill their Kickstarter orders plus produce an additional 1,000 Loomi kits to sell via their website, LoomiLight.com. "It kick-started our business," Hartung says.

Kickstarter users speak: How they set their fund-raising goals

In real life, everyone puts different criteria to work in calculating how much they'll try to raise in a Kickstarter campaign. Worksheets are great tools, but real people are more interesting. Here are some comments from the people behind Kickstarter projects in different creative fields, with various fund-raising targets, explaining how they picked their lucky numbers.

The American Revolution

type: film
goal: $104,000
raised: $114,419

For this documentary about the pioneering Boston rock radio station WBCN, the goal of $104,000 was ambitious but meaningful. New Englanders of a certain (hippie) generation had grown up tuning in to 'BCN at 104 on the FM dial.

"If you took 104 out of the mix, we might have gone for something like 75 [thousand dollars]," says filmmaker Bill Lichtenstein. "It just seemed like such an obvious branding thing. It was an ambitious number. But another filmmaker, Jennifer Fox, had set a goal of $50,000 and blew through it, raising $150,000 for a documentary about Buddhism. "We'd sold 900 tickets for a party, and we figured if we could get 900 'BCN listeners to kick in a hundred bucks, that would be $90,000 right there. If we could get a hundred thousand people to each kick in a dollar . . . With the reach the station had, it seemed reasonable. If we had set a goal of $50,000 and we were at $30,000 with nineteen days to go, we would have been saying, *Why were we so timid?*"

A Year Without Rent

type: film
goal: $12,000
raised: $12,178

Lucas McNelly set his bar at a much more conservative level when seeking money for his film project, in which he proposed to travel around the United States working on independent films and documenting his journey.

"The $12,000 was the minimum I figured I could do it for. That was the minimum I felt I could survive on," McNelly says. "The plan all along was to pick up sponsors, and that didn't pan out the way I thought it would. We thought sponsors would jump on board and run ads. In fact, we later had to have a secondary campaign. A couple of other filmmakers I know started a secondary campaign [ten months into the year] to get me money [an additional $5,397]. The $12,000 would basically cover gas and food and cell phone."

McNelly said he was planning to return to Kickstarter with a new film project and a higher goal, possibly $100,000. It might help to ask for a lot from the start, he thinks. He feels that film projects are different from those Kickstarter projects that promise to deliver tech gadgets or other tangible products to backers. In such cases, people are shopping for stuff, and if they pledge more, the creator makes more. Often those campaigns dramatically exceed the amount the creator asked for. Not so with films.

As he explains: "If you're trying to make a film and you say, *we can do this for $30,000*, it's kind of like an oral contract with your audience. There's no reason to give you $60,000. Especially when there's, like, two dozen other film campaigns running at the same time."

Freaker USA

type: design
goal: $48,500
raised: $63.770

At first glance, the team that brought the world the Freaker, a stylish knit cozy to keep beverage bottles dry and grippable, appears to be a gang of loveable hipsters who just want to party. But their fundraising Kickstarter goal was based on hardcore calculations, according to Freaker inventor Zach Crain:

"We looked at all the numbers, and what we wanted to accomplish with the project, and then we figured out how much the little percentage that Amazon and Kickstarter take would figure out the cost of the product, and then what we would be left with. We came out with the number that would allow us to be left with a little bit of money after we got all the product and could take a step forward with it."

Romo – The Smartphone Robot

type: technology
goal: $32,000
raised: $114,796

The Romotive team, which invented a little tanklike robot that can be controlled by a phone, took a practical business approach, too. Team member Peter Seid explains: "The $32,000 goal was the number at which we thought we could get to some sort of scale in manufacturing."

Detroit Needs A Statue of Robocop!

type: sculpture
goal: $50,000
raised: $67,436

Who knows how much it costs to create and install a statue? The guys who dreamed up this ambitious idea did some smart research before setting their fund-raising target. Team member Brandon Walley offers behind-the-scenes details: "I made some preliminary calls to an art school. I didn't know anything about making a statue. I talked to a couple of people who make large sculptures, and we got a general sense [of cost and manufacturing]. We were thinking the art school might do it in their foundry. We thought maybe we could just get an action figure and make a 3-D scan of that and enlarge it. We figured out it's not gonna be any more than $50,000, so we'll just set that as our goal. If it costs only $25,000, then the extra money could be donated to a park or something where the statue will be installed. Even $50,000—we thought that seemed crazy if we could actually do it. When the campaign went viral and momentum took off, we figured, however much we get, we'll just make the statue as big or as epic as we can."

Gremolata & Cancellaresca Milanese
type: graphic design
goal: $25,000 ("**new goal**": $48,000)
raised: $45,242

If you surpass your all-or-nothing goal, you can informally set new, higher goals and attach new possibilities to them. That's what Russell Maret and Micah Currier did when their project to have a foundry engrave and cast a new metal type family met its goal *on the first day*! Maret explained what happened in an update the pair posted on their project page:

"When Micah and I first decided to try funding this project on Kickstarter, we set our goal at $37,000 so that we could cast 500 lbs. of new type at the end of it. As we got closer to the launch, we lowered our funding goal to $25,000 because it seemed more realistic. After reaching $25,000 on the first day, we decided we might as well try for the whole shebang. Having reached $37,000, there are now new possibilities, like engraving a full set of Romance-language accents or a wider range of ligatured characters. Or simply subsidizing some of the materials I will need to purchase to fulfill the pledges. Either way, we will put the money to good use and make the best, most elaborate typeface we can. Thank you for your support."

Breaking down costs for backers

Once you've decided on a fund-raising target, do you need to tell potential backers exactly how you're going to spend every dollar? The short answer is no. It's not required. You do want them to believe that the money—their money—is necessary for your project and will be spent wisely. Some Kickstarter campaigners have chosen to share a breakdown of expected costs. Such explicit detail can help potential backers feel good about where their money is going.

The creators of the computer game **FTL: Faster Than Light** said in their Kickstarter video that the $10,000 they sought would go toward "the business costs of starting a company, talking to lawyers, stuff like that, and will also allow us to pay our sound designer, which we haven't done yet . . . and it will help us run a closed beta [test]" to work out bugs in the game. They ended up raising $200,542. Pete Taylor, in explaining his $12,000 fund-raising goal for SAVORx, a service to supply backers with fresh spices and spicy recipes, included on his project page an explanation of exactly how much he figured he needed for the different parts of his plan, including even a pie chart and detailed description (*shown right*).

What we need:

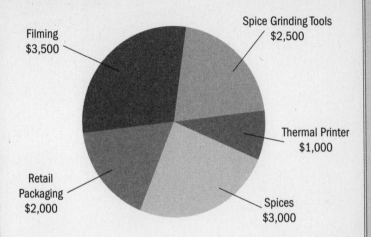

Filming
$3,500

Spice Grinding Tools
$2,500

Thermal Printer
$1,000

Spices
$3,000

Retail
Packaging
$2,000

* Spices, Spices, Spices!!! We have a limited amount of spices right now, but with your help, we can increase how many different spices, rubs, and Recipe Spice Packs we offer! *Cost/$3,000*

* Thermal Printer.... We already have our generic labels, but need a thermal printer to add the specific product details... *Cost/$1,000*

* Retail packaging....We created and sourced our online/web-order packaging, but still need to develop & buy our retail packaging. *We plan on using stackable, square spice tins to help keep your kitchen cabinets CLEAN & ORGANIZED.* I don't know about you, but I hate fishing through the cabinets looking for a bottle of cumin.... EERRGGHHH! *Cost/$2,000*

* Spice Grinding Tools.... We will offer all sorts of Mortar & Pestles, manual spice grinders, and electric spice grinders. Plus some really cool kitchen gadgets/equipment. *Cost/$2,500*

* Film, Film, Film.... We love sharing our passion with others. That is why we create Recipe Spice Pack Videos that show you how to make that dish you really want to try! *Cost/$3,500*

Courtesy Pete Taylor

3.

PLEDGES AND REWARDS

The calculated art of choosing rewards
for your backers

THE CONTRACT YOU ENGAGE IN when you undertake a Kickstarter campaign is pretty straightforward. You're trying to record an album, print a book, finish a film, stage a performance, produce a gadget. You ask your real friends and online friends and kind-hearted strangers to chip in to turn your dream into a reality. Those backers enjoy the sweet satisfaction of knowing they helped you realize your goal. But according to Kickstarter rules, they must also receive a *reward*, a token of appreciation whose value is connected to the amount they donate. This basic transaction is the pumping heart of Kickstarter, and it's one thing you'll want to know everything about before you even embark on your campaign. Setting backer rewards and their corresponding dollar amounts is the most important decision you will make in a Kickstarter campaign. Making the wrong choices (asking for too much or too little pledge money for rewards) can doom a project from the get-go. Worse still, bad planning can turn a successful campaign into a nightmarish experience, especially if the rewards become more costly or difficult to deliver than you bargained for.

You need to understand all the challenges and costs that your rewards will engender before you even set out on your Kickstarter voyage. In this chapter, we will take a closer look at rewards and pledge amounts, examining them from every possible angle and providing lists, charts, and lots of real-life advice from successful Kickstarter campaigns. It might also make sense to skip ahead to chapter 10, "After the Loving—Tales of Fulfillment," which covers the challenges of sending out rewards to backers after a successful campaign. Logistically, that part comes at the end of a campaign, but you'll want to know in advance exactly what you're signing up for when you take people's money and promise them that you'll deliver something tangible in return.

So, what are good pledge amounts and rewards strategies?

In an idealized scenario, the reward your backers receive is a copy of the thing they have pledged to help you create: it's your awesome album of Bollywood music performed solo on a harpsichord, or a DVD of your epic documentary about the World Lawn Mowing Championships, or your dog collar that translates barks and growls into English, or your nifty bicycle-seat clamp that transforms a bike into a bottle opener (this last one was a real Kickstarter project, the **Nectar and Elixir** seat clamps). It's rarely that simple, though. Why? Because there's almost never just one reward. You'll likely need to think up both big rewards and small rewards to encourage big pledges and small pledges, all so that you can persuade everyone to ride along on your magical journey of creation.

Basic Rewards Guidelines

Kickstarter offers guidelines to help you decide on the rewards you'll offer as well as a few hard rules (prohibited rewards) you need to live by. The company breaks rewards into four categories, which provide a useful framework when thinking about what you will offer during your campaign:

* *Copies of the thing*: the album, the DVD, a print from the show; these items should be priced at what they would cost in a retail environment
* *Creative collaborations*: a backer appears as a hero in the comic, everyone gets painted into the mural, two backers do the handclaps for track 3
* *Creative experiences*: a visit to the set, a phone call from the author, dinner with the cast, a concert in your backyard
* *Creative mementos*: photos sent from location, thanks in the credits, meaningful tokens that tell a story

Prohibited Rewards

* Items not directly produced by the project or its creator (i.e., you can't offer things you have in your garage, repackage existing products, etc.)
* Alcohol
* Contests, raffles, lotteries, sweepstakes
* Coupons, discounts, cash-value gift cards
* Financial incentives (ownership, share of profits, repayment)
* Other items on prohibited list (see chapter 1)

source: Kickstarter

Kickstarter has also issued statistics on pledge trends. This bar chart indicates that, overall, as of early 2012 the most popular pledge zone is the $11 to $25 range. Ninety percent of all pledges have been for $100 or less, and 75 percent have been for $50 or less. That makes sense and should factor into not only your rewards ideas but also your overall fund-raising goal.

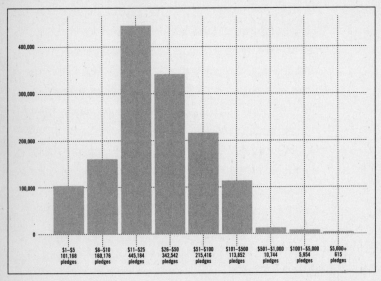

As a practical matter, you'll generally want to offer something for either $1 or $5; some covetable goodies (normally including the product of your project) in the sweet spot from $10 to $100; and some crazy rewards for dream-level backers who want to go all-in. Five different rewards levels seem to suffice for most projects, though many campaign creators end up setting more.

Adding the rewards that will be listed on the page for your Kickstarter project page is easy, once you begin the process of building your campaign on the Kickstarter website (see chapter 7, "The Kickoff!" for more on that part of the process). When you start to build your campaign, a rewards screen is one of the first set-up pages you'll see. For the first reward, you type in a dollar amount, indicate whether only a limited number will be available, add a short but appealing description of the reward, and indicate its expected delivery date. Click on Add Another Backer Reward to do just that, continuing to add rewards until you've reached your decided-upon number. After you've input all of them, hit Save. You can change the information at any time before the campaign is approved by Kickstarter—but then beware: after the project goes live, a pledge amount and its reward description become frozen as soon as one person chooses it. If there's any ambiguity about a reward description and that reward has already been frozen, the campaign creator can clarify questions by using the FAQ that is part of a Kickstarter campaign page or by posting update messages. Either of those can be appended anytime.

The highs and lows of rewards

If the product you're trying to create is especially expensive or especially cheap, then you have covered one end of the pledge-amount spectrum. The other end of the spectrum may require some creative thinking. Consider the **Printrbot**. In late 2011, Brook Drumm used Kickstarter to raise money to sell what he called "your first 3-D printer." It was a kit to build an entry-level machine that would let anyone "print" fully formed three-dimensional plastic objects based on computer designs. This futuristic technology isn't mainstream yet. High-end 3-D printers used in industrial applications cost tens of thousands of dollars. Even this lower-cost version isn't cheap. The lowest pledge level that could reasonably be set for a Printrbot kit on Kickstarter was $499. Which meant that the campaign had its expensive pledge level decided. But what about people who wanted to give a small amount, just to help the campaign but without buying the big-ticket item? Your friends at work, though eager to chip in, might not all need 3-D printers at five hundred bucks a pop. What if someone wanted to give a more modest amount? Well, Drumm took care of that possibility, too. For $10, a backer was entitled to receive a 3-D printed Curvy Coin-Op Bottle opener, and, for $25, the backer would get not only the opener but also a 3-D-printed Printrbot logo keychain.

The opposite problem was encountered by the folks who created the **Freaker**. This knitted beer coozy, a one-size-fits-all "sock" that slips over bottles and cans, does the usual coozy job of soaking up condensation on the outside of a container. The Freaker team offered the product in a variety of awesome designs, from a red, white, and blue American-flag theme to a Charlie Brown shirt zigzag design. A Freaker is extremely inexpensive to make, and the Kickstarter campaign offered to ship one to anyone who pledged just $1.

That's a fabulous offer. But if you're giving away the product for a buck, where do you go from there? How do you attract a $100 pledge—offer a hundred beer coozies? Freaker's rewards structure had to be creative: $1 for a random Freaker; $25 for four random Freakers, and $55 for eight Freakers that a backer could choose. Still, how did the Freaker team get a pledge at the "$2,000 or more" level? They went totally off the charts. They turned a box truck into a Freaker-mobile and offered to bring a "grilled-cheese party" to a location of the backer's choice.

Some backers who come to Kickstarter are looking for prerelease bargains. They expect to pay less than the retail price that will be charged later for the same product. Take the **Loog Guitar**, a wooden kit for making a three-string children's guitar. In April 2011, New York designer/musician Rafael Atijas ran a Kickstarter campaign offering, for $150, a guitar kit that, he said, would sell online later for $215 (it did). He got 308 backers at that pledge level—his most popular level— and raised more than $65,000 after asking for only $15,000. The **TikTok+LunaTik** wristwatch kits were also offered on Kickstarter at early-bird prices. Backers could pledge $25 to get a TikTok that would later sell for $34.95 (2,432 people chose this reward level). Or they could pledge $50 to get a fancier LunaTik that would later sell for $69.95. That bargain got more than 5,000 backers!

But what if you're raising money to create a phone app that you plan to sell for $10 or less when it's done? Can you really ask your earliest backers and closest friends to pledge $25 or $50—essentially overpaying—for it? Here, too, you need to get creative. Your early backers, in the role of generous patrons and supporters, might be willing to give $50 and just get the app as a thank-you. After all, we've been trained by public-broadcasting pledge drives to donate $120 for a VHS tape of old crooners.

For most creators, the purpose of Kickstarter is not to make a killing on a creation but to get it done, and hopefully fully funded. Many creators find a middle ground that covers costs and, depending on the donor response, may leave a little extra funding to grow on. A Seattle start-up company called Romotive went to Kickstarter to fund the development of **Romo**, a small, tanklike plastic vehicle that could be controlled like a robot by a ride-along Android smartphone. They offered the kit for a $78 pledge—and that was the most popular pledge level, attracting 800 backers. In all, they raised $114,796, but they had a lot of robots to send out afterward.

"Our Kickstarter campaign wasn't about trying to raise a ton of money," said Peter Seid of Romotive after the campaign but before the reward robots were shipped. "Seventy-eight dollars is not that much for what we're giving people. I don't think it's gonna be a loss, but it's not like we're making fifty bucks a robot or anything." In fact, the real payoff really came after the campaign, when Romotive began selling Romo kits to the public from its website.

Rewards ideas for everyone

Are you stumped for reward ideas? Assembled here is a table full of inspirational ideas for each of the thirteen Kickstarter categories, based on actual stuff offered by successful campaigns. Get creative, adapting these ideas or expanding on them to suit your own project.

Kickstarter Award Ideas by Creative Category

Category	Entry-Level Reward
Film	digital download of film, DVD, name in "thank you" crawl in credits, behind-the-scenes photos, soundtrack music, T-shirts, mugs
Music	digital download of the music, CD, T-shirt, poster
Design	product accessories, actual product (low cost)
Art	digital version of artwork, physical artwork (very small), art on T-shirt, mug, postcards, poker chips, calendar
Publishing	e-books, paperbacks, magazine issues, subscriptions, T-shirts, mugs
Technology	project-related T-shirts, stickers, decals, product accessories
Theater	CD or DVD, show program, poster
Games	copy of game (digital apps), listing in credits, game accessories, T-shirts
Food	recipes, food, foodie implements and accessories
Photography	digital images, inkjet prints, images on T-shirts, photo book (inexpensive)
Comics	stickers, decals, T-shirts and other items with comic art, digital comics, or special Web access, backer thanks in graphic novels
Fashion	print, T-shirt, tote bag, mug related to garment designs
Dance	credit in performance literature or on website, tote bag, T-shirt, poster, digital video

Midlevel Reward	High-End Reward
"producer" credit, movie poster, autographed script or photo, screening or party invitation	appear as an extra in the movie, spend the day as director's assistant, phone or Skype call with director or actors, iPad with the movie preloaded on it, personal screening
signed CDs, name in CD liner notes, handwritten lyrics, release party invitation, admission to invitation-only performance	name on the tour van, customized song for the backer, music or vocal lesson, DJ'd party at your house, private concert
actual product (midcost), multiple products, product with accessory package, product with color or feature selection	actual product (high cost), multiple products, highly customized or limited editions, personal visit to install or set up product
artwork (small to medium), art book, print or giclée of original painting, backers-only gallery opening	Large art piece, custom made art, art lesson, day with the artist, portrait of backer by the artist, exclusive opening or reception, personal visit/exhibition from artist (large/mobile installations)
hardcover edition, autographed copies, poster, hoodie	conference workshop passes, launch party invitations, time or chat with book author, chance to guest-edit or contribute content to magazine
midpriced product produced in the project	high-end product produced by the Kickstarter campaign, assembled version of DIY kit, customized versions
tickets to rehearsal or performance	invitation to party or reception, behind-the-scenes access to production, acting class
copy of board game or computer/video game, USB thumb drive containing game rules	custom or original artwork, access to closed beta test, backer name or image in the game, naming rights to objects in the game, "our products for life"
cookbook, more food, cooking class, restaurant meal	offer to plan meal/choose wine for backer, create custom food item, prepare and serve a meal on location, personal cooking lesson
framed and unframed photo prints, high-end or signed photo book	photography lesson, personal photo shoot, exclusive gallery opening or reception invitation
hardcopy books, USB thumb drive containing digital versions, signed posters	original artwork, personalized illustration by artist, your character drawn into the comic
midpriced garment created by the Kickstarter project	high-end garment, custom-fit garment, garment named after the backer
DVD of performance, rehearsal admission, entry to group dance class, garment or prop used in performance	private dance lesson, consultation with a show seamstress, exclusive performance tickets, choreography of backer's event, personal dance performance

We do it all for you: Some personalized rewards

Because you can never have too many ideas for cool rewards, here are some specific, highly personalized ones offered by real-life Kickstarter creators.

campaign: Authors, Publishers and Readers of Independent Literature

pledge amount: $35 or more

reward: "Reverse Fan Mail—We'll send your name or a name of your choice to one of our favorite independent-press authors, who will write a short original piece with that name as the inspiration."

campaign: Nano Whitman – an album, a tour

pledge amount: $100 or more

reward: Your name on the van that the band took on tour. "I put like forty names on my van," Whitman says. "I got so many $100 hits. I think if I had a less compelling gift in that spot, I wouldn't have made it. I think it stretched people's donation level a little, the difference between the $50 and $100 to get your name on my van."

campaign: Krochet Kids Peru: limited edition hat collection

pledge amount: $1,000 or more

reward: "Get a new hat style named after you. Imagine 'the Eric,' 'the Jennifer,' or 'the Peggy' roaming the globe on the heads of KKi supporters."

campaign: Freaker USA—Making You & Your Beverage Cooler!

pledge amount: $2,000 or more

reward: BBQ party for you and your friends (or if a town collectively pledges $3,000, a grilled cheese party!).

campaign: Backhausdance is Performing in New York at Joyce SoHo
pledge amount: $5,000 or more
reward: Jennifer Backhaus and an assistant will "fly anywhere in the U.S. and spend the day with the cast of your choosing to set choreography for your event."

campaign: The Order of the Stick Reprint Drive
pledge amount: $5,000 or more
reward: "Your original D&D character, based on your descriptions (within reason), gets a walk-on cameo in The Order of the Stick webcomic sometime this year." Plus, an original, signed crayon drawing of the character, and other goodies.

Can you offer a tax deduction for pledges?

Some Kickstarter campaigns promise backers that their pledge dollars will be tax deductible. That's definitely an incentive to give. But it's not something you can set up through Kickstarter. In order for pledges to be tax deductible, you need to be a legitimate charity in the eyes of U.S. tax collectors. That requires becoming a federally approved nonprofit organization, technically, a 501(c)(3). This is done by filing paperwork with the U.S. Internal Revenue Service. You need to submit an application (which isn't guaranteed to be approved) that contains a mission statement explaining the purpose of your organization as well as its bylaws; in addition, you'll need to create a board of directors. Nonprofits must file ongoing tax returns. So becoming a nonprofit isn't something you do just for kicks. Many resources on the process are available online, including searches at IRS.gov for information about 501(c)(3) status and rules, Publication 557, and Form 1023. If you decide to go this route, you will probably want to involve an accountant, a lawyer, or both.

An alternative is to try a program (separate from Kickstarter) through which arts fund-raisers can affiliate themselves with existing nonprofit organization to receive tax-deductible donations. Some of these are listed in chapter 12.

The most important equation: Matching rewards to pledge levels

Once you've identified rewards that make sense for your campaign, it's time to do some hardcore research and serious financial math. You need to know, as precisely as possible, what it will cost you to make and deliver each item listed in your rewards. That means the real cash cost, which you can use with the worksheets provided in chapter 2. For practical purposes, it could also factor in your time and opportunity cost (time taken away from your other work). Matching your rewards to pledge levels that are fair to your backers and worthwhile for you can be a major challenge. Keep in mind that, in general, the most popular pledge level will be the one at which a backer can get The Thing, whatever your thing is, whether it's a gadget that you've invented or a DVD of a movie.

It's easy to calculate poorly. Matt Haughey, a tech pioneer who by early 2012 had backed more than eighty-five Kickstarter projects, has seen it all: "Use the numbers wisely," he says. "Don't have $5 rewards that give people the thing. If you want thousands of dollars, you'll never get there five dollars at a time." In general, you want to cut your losses before they have a chance to start. Little things can catch you by surprise, such as the extra cost of international shipping. One of Kickstarter's most highly funded art projects was a groovy vinyl record album of the **Tell Em Steve Dave** podcast. The project asked for $6,500 and received $61,218 from 2,040 backers—788 of those backers were from overseas. Fortunately, the creators had set up their rewards system the right way: backers in the United States could pledge $26 pledge to receive a copy of the record, while those with an international shipping requirement needed to pledge $35 for the same reward.

Nathaniel Hansen, a Boston filmmaker who has been involved with more than a dozen Kickstarter projects, has advised taking an even more severe policy toward the hassles and costs of shipping: "I try not to put anything in the mail for under $50." To that somewhat mercenary rule-of-thumb, allow us to add another caveat: Don't offer any individually customized reward for under $100. Haughey offers the important reminder that your time is valuable, too. "I've seen people offer 'a Skype conversation with me,' and then twenty or thirty people choose that! The person then has like six hours of Skype conversations to do."

Sometimes Kickstarter campaigners have been happily surprised by the number of high-end rewards their most passionate backers go in for. Yehuda Berlinger, founder of the board-game website Purple Pawn, wrote in a summary of his Kickstarter research that "early-adopting gamers—the ones you are trying to court—are loyal, fervent, communicative, know a lot about what makes a good game, and have cash to spend but don't want to be cheated. They don't spend $1 to get a 'thanks,' but they will spend $25 to $40 without much thought on a board game if they think that they'll get a quality game. They'll regularly drop more money ($250+) in exchange for special perks."

Gary Sarli, a game developer in Denton, Texas, who raised $14,605 on Kickstarter for his **e20: System Evolved** role-playing game, has blogged about his experience and remarked on just how careful you need to be in matching rewards with pledge levels. He offered a hypothetical scenario in which someone might be trying to raise $5,000 using three pledge/reward levels: a PDF of a game rule book for $10, a printed paperback of the rule book for $25, and an autographed hardcover plus other perks for $100. The possible aftermath of this reward mix is eye-opening. If you were to reach $5,000 by selling 500 of the $10 PDFs, your cost is close to nothing to deliver the all-digital rewards. That's great—if you can get 500 people. If you had reached the $5,000 goal by selling 200 of the $25 paperback books, your printing cost could run $4.50 to $6 per book, and, after adding in shipping costs, you might spend $10 per book, or $2,000 total to deliver the goods. That's not so great. Finally, if you receive 50 of the $100 pledges to reach your goal, your cost might be somewhere in between, maybe $15 per book, for $750 total.

Of course, you're sure to get a mix of pledge levels. But pledge levels can be thrown surprisingly out of balance if one seems to be a much better deal than another. "Depending on which reward levels people choose, your ultimate costs can fluctuate dramatically," Sarli notes. He advises all Kickstarter campaigners to "plan and budget for the worst-case [highest-cost] scenario."

For similar planning purposes, Sarli also warns against bundling several projects together into one Kickstarter campaign and then letting backers choose which ones they want as a reward. That can lead to disaster, he says. What if your rewards include a game rule book and a novel based on your game's characters—and then just one backer chooses the novel as a reward? He points out that you'd have to write the whole novel for one person!

And it's not cheating to pretest your rewards and pledge levels before you even put them on Kickstarter. It's called homework. The computer game developers at inXile Entertainment, before seeking funding for their **Wasteland 2** game on Kickstarter, started a discussion thread in the user forum on the company website, posting twelve proposed rewards attached to pledges ranging from $15 to $10,000. They asked fans for feedback and made a few adjustments before launching their Kickstarter campaign. Similarly, Daniel Solis, a game developer in Durham, North Carolina, posted on his website a list of proposed rewards and pledge levels before launching a

Kickstarter for his dice game **Utara**. "We're gradually refining the reward tiers for the upcoming Utara Kickstarter campaign," he wrote, and allowed his fans to comment and ask questions. That's a terrific way to gauge interest and get it right before making any costly commitments.

Adding rewards during a campaign

Be prepared to get creative and add rewards during a campaign if a project is unexpectedly successful or you see an untapped opportunity to appeal to a new set of backers. **The Order of the Stick Reprint Drive**, an early 2012 Kickstarter campaign by Philadelphia illustrator Rich Burlew to reprint books of his popular webcomics, exploded so rapidly that Burlew had to keep frantically adding pledge levels and rewards, almost daily, as nearly 15,000 backers raided his inventory of existing books and many items sold out. He ended up with about seventy different pledge levels/rewards—and raised more than $1.2 million!

"I was tragically underprepared," Burlew said in an interview on the Kickstarter blog. "I would have set up my rewards packages differently. They're a mess, largely because I didn't want to put up any books as a reward that I might not have gotten enough funds to reprint—and because I can't edit any reward once a backer has chosen it."

Pete Taylor, a chef in Spokane, Washington, got creative when adding rewards to his **SAVORx** campaign to distribute fresh spices and recipes to backers after he realized a particular type of reward was missing.

"Two-thirds of the way into the campaign, I noticed I didn't have a lot of local-value rewards," he says. "So I added a one-on-one cooking lesson. I offered a 'Spice Makeover,' where I'd go into your house and rip out all your old, nasty spices and replace them with whole spices. And I offered the 'Exquisite Dinner,' where we plan out a menu, and I go shopping for the ingredients, cook at your house for as many people as you want to invite, clean up, and get out of there. That was for $325 [cost of food not included]. Four people pledged that. They're all based in the Spokane area. So I've got a lot of work cut out for me in the next six months!"

You can also limit rewards during a campaign. If 395 people have made pledges that will get them one of your fancy artisan potholders, and you've realized that you can't produce more than 400 of them, you can set the limit at 400 before the pledges surpass that number. A reward that is reaching its available limit is marked as "sold out." Probably the highest-profile case of limiting rewards is the incredible Pebble project, which raised more than $10 million on Kickstarter in April and May of 2012. The creators of the ultrastylish "smart" wristwatch set one key limit from the start: as an early-bird special, they made 200 watches available for only $99. After those quickly sold out, backers needed to pledge $115 to get a Pebble watch. When the project completely exploded, with more than 67,000 backers jumping onboard, the creators chose to set every reward as "sold out," essentially ceasing their fund-raising nearly two weeks before the scheduled end of their campaign.

The littlest pledge: Getting creative with the $1 reward

Backers are always free to donate $1 to your Kickstarter project, even if your least expensive reward requires a $2 or $5 pledge. Of course, you won't get rich on dollar pledges, and some project creators simply ignore the category altogether. Here's why you shouldn't.

"I don't get why people don't do the $1 reward more. It's just like spitting in people's faces to ignore it," says filmmaker Lucas McNelly, whose **A Year Without Rent** project ended successfully in early 2011. "It doesn't cost you anything. For the people who give you $1, you still have their e-mail address. And they can become your biggest fans! They may drag six people to the theater to see your movie."

Most often, project creators offer "hearty thanks" or "sincere gratitude" for the one-buck pledge. Sometimes they'll post your $1-giving name on Facebook or Twitter or in the credits to their project. In rare cases, as with the **Freaker**, creators give out the product itself—but that's rare.

McNelly had a great $1 reward: "Good karma. You can never have too much of that. Everyone gets this, even if they opt out." Bill Lichtenstein, a Boston filmmaker, raised $114,419 to make **"The American Revolution,"** a documentary about the pioneering FM radio station WBCN. He agrees that collecting many small donations is crucial. "Groupon doesn't want one guy buying a thousand coupons. They want to build a customer base," he points out. His $1 reward was "cosmic good vibes, our exclusive project updates, and our sincere thank you in the film's closing credits." He was serious about including everyone in a thank-you crawl in his film: "My thought was that, in the spirit of the radio station, anybody who helps should get a thank-you. Even if the credits go on for five minutes."

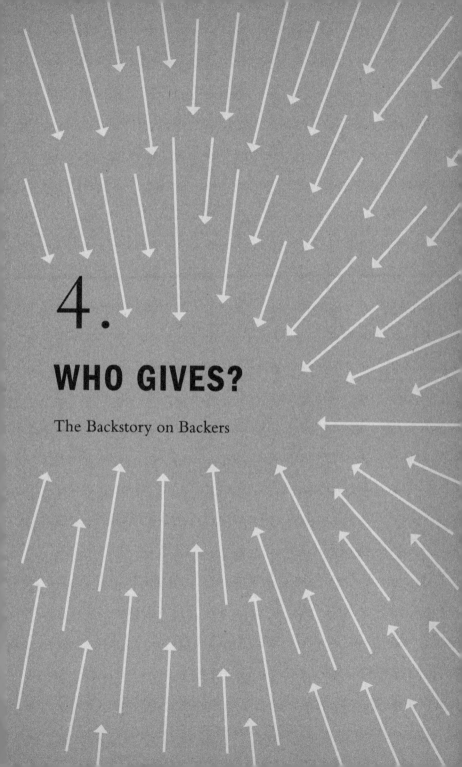

4.

WHO GIVES?

The Backstory on Backers

B Y NOW, WE'VE ESTABLISHED that Kickstarter isn't a magical honey pot where you can just post a project and count on swarms of random people showing up, tossing thousands of dollars into it. It just doesn't work that way. Yes, there are some frequent backers who bestow pledges on a project just because it's cool, or they use Kickstarter as a sort of early-adopter gift shop (see the interview with Matt Haughey, page 80). But munificent strangers who spend their days lavishing wealth upon Kickstarter projects are rare and, generally speaking, will not get your project funded. According to statistics that Kickstarter released in late 2011, only 16 percent of all funders up to that time were "repeat backers" who had given to more than one project. That means the vast majority had given to only one project. It's likely that, for most of the people who support your project financially, it will be the only one they fund. One hard truth of crowdfunding is that you'll have to supply your own crowd.

Here's the counterintuitive part, though. The most obvious alternatives to unknown benefactors—meaning, your closest family members and dearest friends—aren't a major funding source in a lot of Kickstarter campaigns, either. "Everybody talks about how, oh, it's just your friends and your family who back you," says Lucas

McNelly, a filmmaker who raised $12,172 for a project called **A Year Without Rent**. "I've now had three campaigns—the two that I ran and then a secondary Year Without Rent campaign [managed by his friends]. And I've yet to get a dollar from anyone related to me." Scott Thrift had a similar experience. "Ninety percent of the people who bought the clock, I have no clue who they are," says Thrift, who raised $97,567 to produce his one-year clock called **The Present**.

So, then, who does that leave to fund your project? Mostly, it seems, the core of pledge dollars come from a middle ground of backers that you need to assemble and rally, people who are part of your extended network, acquaintances, those connected to your acquaintances by multiple degrees of separation. They're strangers who may already be fans either of your work or of the genre you're working in. They're people who share your passion whom you've never met before, but you're able to pull them in by making connections as well as by getting mentioned in the media outlets they pay attention to.

"Friends and family helped out the least," says Pete Taylor, who raised $12,710 for a foodie project called **SAVORx**. "Maybe it's just me. Acquaintances helped out a decent amount. And total strangers. I found out that with all the networking and all the promotion through Facebook, Twitter, cold-calling, e-mailing, however many thousands of e-mails I sent, the response was that family and friends are less likely to pledge than people you know just a tiny bit. Maybe you're sort of friends with them on Facebook. Small-business owners, corporate-type individuals, marketers, social media people, they're the ones who really supported the campaign. I didn't have one family member go to our fund-raising event, but I had probably thirty people I'd never met in my life show up."

Bill Lichtenstein, a Boston-based filmmaker who worked his contacts relentlessly to raise $114,419 on Kickstarter to make **The American Revolution**, a documentary about pioneering FM rock station WBCN, breaks the types of backers into tiers.

"First responders are those with direct involvement," he says. In his case, they were individuals who had some direct association with Lichtenstein or the legendary radio station and were early to jump in to support the project. "Next tier is outsiders who are fans." In the case of a radio station with a regional reach, a wide, multigenerational set of fans might be intrigued by a film project about the station they grew up listening to. In your own case, they could be fans of your blog or people who share your abiding passion for, say, oil paintings of tortoises. "There are tons of people who might be predisposed to giving $10, $25, but you have to get to them," Lichtenstein says. "You have to ask them. Give them a clear path to do it, and that's really the hard part. The divide between a person physically getting out a credit card and making a donation, it's a big jump."

Since you need to draw a crowd, it's critical to consider where they will come from. What is your constituency, your community? What do these folks have in common? Is it where they live—is yours a local project, such as a bringing comedy festival to your city, erecting a statue on a downtown square, or celebrating a beloved radio station? Is it a specialized interest that cuts across people around the nation or the world? Scott Thrift's time-savoring one-year clock appealed to people worldwide who shared his sensibility, and maybe his design sense, too. "My project was really unique because it is global. It appeals to the human being, beyond race or nationality or age," Thrift says. By contrast, Abbey Londer was raising money for a comedy festival called **RIOT**, which would be based in Los Angeles. "Initially, most of the funds came from the comedy community in Los Angeles," she confirms.

Nevertheless, some Kickstarter projects with essentially local interest have succeeded in appealing to a wider audience beyond the one concerned in the campaign. The **Detroit Needs A Statue of Robocop!** campaign in early 2011 attracted pledges from *RoboCop* movie fanatics the world over, many of whom might never set foot in Detroit. This success proves that some things are just too cool to stay local.

Some backer statistics

In October 2011 the Kickstarter website announced an amazing number. It had reached one million backers. A million people around the world had pledged money to one or more Kickstarter campaigns. At about the same time, the grand total of funds pledged on Kickstarter passed the $100 million mark.

The way the math works, every backer can be said to represent $100 in pledges. Kickstarter's data gurus broke it down more scientifically: those one million backers had posted a total of roughly 1.4 million pledges, or 1.4 per person on average. Thus the average pledge amount was about $71. So if the average backer makes 1.4 pledges of $71, he's in for roughly a hundred bucks. But though $71 is the average, the most common pledge amount is in fact $30, according to Kickstarter.

Every project creator, once a campaign begins, gets to see a dashboard containing information about where backers are coming from, including a big-picture pie chart like the one shown here (*opposite*). This particular chart, which comes from a successful 2011 campaign, shows that 89 percent of the funding came from people referred to the project page from *outside* Kickstarter—that is, from e-mail or Facebook or a blog or other media link. Only 11 percent started at the project page itself or came from another part of Kickstarter, such as a page that highlights particular projects. That 8-to-1 ratio is a high proportion, but not atypical. If you visit Kickstarter thinking your funding will be mostly from people who are browsing the site looking for cool stuff, you may end up disappointed—and underfunded.

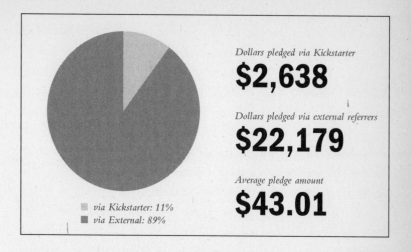

Dollars pledged via Kickstarter

$2,638

Dollars pledged via external referrers

$22,179

Average pledge amount

$43.01

via Kickstarter: 11%
via External: 89%

Sources of pledges for a genuine Kickstarter campaign

A more detailed table on the Kickstarter dashboard itemizes exactly from what sites backers are coming, breaking down the top twenty-five "referring sources." As an example, a 2012 comic project on Kickstarter called **Goats Book IV: Inhuman Resources** published statistics about its backers and how they came to land on the campaign page: 14.7 percent were from Twitter, 9.6 percent from Facebook, 2.69 percent from the blog Boing Boing, and 19 percent from amultiverse.com, which is the website of the project's creator, illustrator Jonathan Rosenberg. These data suggest that a major source of funding is people who are already fans of the artist.

One other statistic that's worth noting: although 46 percent of Kickstarter projects are successful, 89 percent of all backers have supported a successful project, and about 85 percent of pledges are to successfully funded projects. That makes sense in a self-fulfilling sort of way: the reason successful projects are successful is because they attract more backers. Kickstarter puts it this way: "The overwhelming experience of a Kickstarter backer is success."

White knights and big kahunas

Many Kickstarter campaigns have succeeded thanks to the assistance of large donors lined up in advance, individuals who are prepared to kick in $1,000 or $5,000 or more to push a campaign into winning territory. Truth be told, strategic use of the big kahuna, the white knight, the great white whale—whatever you want to call it—is sometimes part of playing the Kickstarter game. (Pete Taylor calls his big donor a "floater," and he took that backer's large pledge midway through his campaign to give it momentum.) A whale's promise to donate a chunk of money may be contingent, *a pledge to pledge*. Kickstarter prohibits project creators from pledging to their own campaigns, but if you're only $2,000 shy of success in a campaign to raise $50,000, everyone understands that it would be crazy to leave that money on the table. Maybe your father or brother-in-law or aunt will offer to pitch in the last bit of money needed to send you into the end zone, saving you from forfeiting the $48,000 you've already raised. Maybe you'll promise to repay the person later. This strategy is not quite true to the spirit of Kickstarter, but it's not prohibited, either. It's a victimless crime. No one gets hurt, and everyone ends up happy. The people who pledged to your project do want it to succeed, after all. The folks at Kickstarter want it to succeed, too.

Capturing the great white whale is often about the people you know. Bill Lichtenstein, a longtime player in the Boston media and music scenes, was able to convince Peter Wolf, lead singer of the J. Geils Band, to offer himself as a reward during Lichtenstein's campaign for the WBCN radio-station documentary. Lichtenstein also got lucky when Jonathan Kraft, owner of the New England Patriots football team, donated $5,000 and went on a pregame radio show to talk about Lichtenstein's Kickstarter campaign.

The partners behind the Detroit RoboCop statue got a surprising "big kahuna" message on day two of their campaign to raise $50,000.

A businessman wrote to say that as soon as they hit the $25,000 mark, he would be willing to pledge the rest. The donor was exactly the right guy for the job. Pete Hotelet runs a company called Omni Consumer Products, through which he takes items that originated in movies (like the Stay Puft Marshmallows from *Ghostbusters* and Brawndo energy drink from *Idiocracy*) and works with movie studios to turn them into real products.

"I thought it was a joke at first," says Brandon Walley, a partner in that Kickstarter campaign. "But he was legit. We had to reach out to Kickstarter to see if they were OK with his offer. It was kind of unprecedented for them [Kickstarter's single pledge limit is $10,000]. It was day six when we hit $25,000, and then I think Pete ended up calling Kickstarter directly with his American Express card." Did the RoboCop statue guys ever consider having Hotelet make his donation to the effort offline? "We talked about that: let the campaign go, and you can match after it's done," Walley says. "But then maybe we wouldn't reach the fifty grand, and then we wouldn't get any of it."

Abbey Londer, who raised money for the **RIOT** comedy festival, had several successful entertainers participate in her Kickstarter video. Theoretically, many of them could have become a big kahuna, pitching in with a donation large enough to cover most or all of her Kickstarter campaign. "I've had a couple of people say, 'If you fall short, we'll give you whatever you need,'" Londer acknowledged midway through her Kickstarter effort. "But that's not happening. Everybody's chipped in."

Despite the attraction of luring a big kahuna, many Kickstarter creators feel that widespread support is preferable, especially for the long-term prospects of a project after a campaign effort is over. Part of what you achieve on Kickstarter is public awareness. You attract an audience for your product, your film, your book, your artwork. Says filmmaker Lucas McNelly: "I was telling people that I would rather have twelve thousand $1 backers than one $20,000 backer. Because I needed that audience. I equate it to playing poker in a casino. You can't play against the same six people every day and expect to make a profit because you'll just be trading the same money back and forth among the same players. People complain about celebrities doing Kickstarter campaigns, and I'm like, don't you get it? They're bringing more people into the casino. They're introducing more people to Kickstarter, and those people may eventually find their way to your campaign."

Meet Matt Haughey

Matt Haughey, backer extraordinaire

Matt Haughey is one of those mythical beings: the mysterious benefactor who will pledge money to a Kickstarter project just because he thinks it's cool, even if he doesn't know the creator personally. As of March 2012, Haughey had backed eighty-four projects (and almost all of them ended up successfully funded). As an online entrepreneur himself—he created the crowdsourced news site MetaFilter—he appreciates the power of the Web to bring people and ideas together, and he loves the Kickstarter concept. "I feel that artists shouldn't have to pay for paint. Inspiration should be the limiting factor in art, not cost," he says. (Through a mutual connection, he became a "very small" [his words] early investor in Kickstarter, but definitely does not speak for the company.)

Still, Haughey doesn't toss his cash around like Floyd Mayweather Jr. Rather, he uses Kickstarter for his own benefit, and he has some specific ideas about what a project creator should do to attract backers like him. He was kind enough to consent to an interview.

You wrote a post on your blog (a.wholelottanothing.org) saying that you use Kickstarter almost like a gift shop. That is, if cool products are being offered, especially if the campaigns are ending soon, you'll kick in $20 or $40 to get a neat gizmo shipped to your door.

Haughey: Yeah. I have something showing up from a Kickstarter project, like, every week. The site is trying to move away from: *it's a store, and I bought something.* They still want it to be: *I'm pledging $50 in the hopes that this guy makes this thing.* But the product stuff is just like a store. It's like, *I made this toy. Here's one of them. I'm gonna make a thousand of them if I get this much money.* Maybe once a month I go to the Ending Soon page and treat it like a store.

How else do you learn about projects that you might back?

Haughey: People are obsessed with *how are backers gonna find me?* Most of my discoveries are made through Twitter. I have a bunch of creative friends; I follow five hundred people and have about ten thousand followers. People will just say, *check out this crazy new thing on Kickstarter.* So that's the principal way I find out about these projects. A lot of it is just absolute luck, serendipity. I really don't browse Kickstarter's site too much. They send out a weekly e-mail that's highly curated: *here are our favorite projects this week.* Those are almost always amazing, and I almost always back one of them every week. Also, I'm a big cyclist, so friends who run biking blogs scour Kickstarter for any bike-related things.

Do people solicit you directly for their Kickstarter campaigns?

Haughey: I'm getting phone calls almost once a day from random people. They just want help. I've gotten some weird hate mail, too, from people who can't stand Kickstarter.

Why?

Haughey: The first thing they tell you at Kickstarter is to leverage your own network. But people are like, *I came to Kickstarter so they would give me free money!*

That's an easy misconception to have but the first one that should be tossed out the window . . .

Haughey: A lot of people think that being on Kickstarter will automatically get them something. It helps to have some sort of network. It helps to have fans already. It's true that there have been compelling "nobodies," too. That guy with the iPhone dock who raised more than a million dollars [Casey Hopkins's Elevation Dock]. I had never heard of the guy. He had a great video, and it's the best idea in the world for anybody with an iPhone charger next to the bed that's flimsy and plastic. A heavy, metal one would be great.

His video showed the product being manufactured and working. That helps.

Haughey: If I'm gonna give money to some random guy, the idea has to be amazing. It's hard to tell people, *Step One is: Have a Really Amazing Idea*, because that's hard. But the flip side is: demonstrate expertise to people. For all the product stuff, I like to see prototypes instead of just ideas or drawings. Anyone can spit out a 3-D CAD drawing. It doesn't really mean anything. It gives no idea whether the person is capable of building it. The people who are most successful, they have a prototype, the design is nailed down. They just need to ramp up tooling or pay a factory to make a lot more.

What if I'm making not a product but an artwork?

Haughey: It helps to be viewed as an expert somehow. It helps to have an online presence. Even if you just have a blog about whatever thing you're creating. Just so people understand what your expertise is. If you're gonna do a photo project, show me something you've done. This may be this guy's first book or album or iPhone accessory, but what else has he done?

A person contacted me who was writing a financial advice book. It sounded like good stuff, how there's terrible financial education in America. The person proposed writing a book about how to be an adult. It sounded awesome. But I hadn't seen anything else this person has written. So I said, *why don't you seek out blogs?* The Web has a million finance blogs. People are always starving for free content. So write a guest post. Offer chapter 1 to finance blogs. And at the end you can plug your Kickstarter. That's a super-easy connection you can make to get your name out there.

So it's called crowdfunding, but even with benefactors like you, people still need to bring their own crowd.

Haughey: It helps to have fans. The biggest success predictor for me is Twitter feeds. If a person is following twenty people and is followed by five people, and they're asking for $15,000 for a book that isn't written, they end up raising $100 and that's it. If your blog has five hundred followers, you're going to be cashing in lots of goodwill, asking people for money.

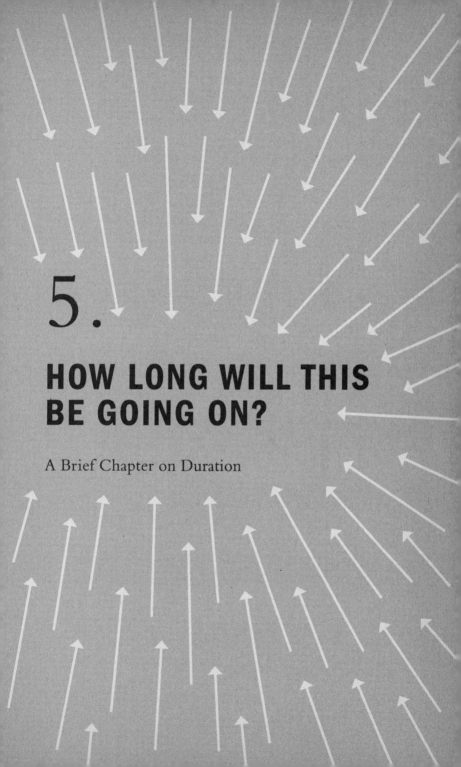

5.

HOW LONG WILL THIS BE GOING ON?

A Brief Chapter on Duration

I N MID-2011, the bosses at Kickstarter looked at data from every Kickstarter campaign for the prior two years and made a surprising discovery: the projects that had given themselves the most time to reach a funding goal had reached their goal least often. At the time, 44 percent of all projects had succeeded (that percentage has since risen to 46). But only 24 percent of ninety-day campaigns had succeeded, despite having had more time to work their magic. Kickstarter's data analysts didn't have a completely scientific explanation for this phenomenon. It was unclear what was a cause and what was an effect. Do longer campaigns fail because they're long? Kickstarter's blog hypothesized that a long campaign may seem less urgent—the duration "makes it easier for backers to procrastinate, and sometimes they forget to come back at all." Or do longer campaigns fail because their creators are less confident to begin with, and maybe the projects aren't rock-solid ideas?

It's an upside-down phenomenon that is hard to explain. But the Kickstarter brass insists it's true. Based on their findings, they took an immediate step: they shortened the maximum duration of a campaign from ninety days to sixty. And they recommended thirty days as the ideal length.

How long should your campaign be? We recommend thirty days,

too. The Kickstarter blog shared a chart that shows the point in a campaign when the most pledges occur. The answer: at the beginning and the end, regardless of the campaign's duration. It's common for campaigns to experience an initial spurt in donations (**Elevation Dock**, an elegant iPhone dock, raised $165,910 in its first twenty-four hours), followed by a lull, and then a closing surge. So the chart is a big letter U, with a trough in the middle representing the slow midcampaign grind.

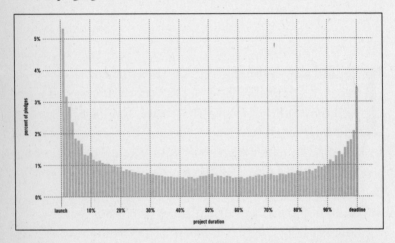

Once again, we'll supplement cold, hard statistical data with real-world advice from successful Kickstarter creators. What follows are a few words from people describing how they chose their campaign duration:

RIOT—L.A.'s Alternative Comedy Festival
raised $22,380 in 30 days
Abbey Londer, the comedy show promoter behind this Kickstarter campaign, says: "We did thirty days. We thought: $20,000 is a lot of money, we need at least thirty days. We didn't expect the amount of feedback and attention that we got. If we could do it again, I might do it in just twenty days, to be honest. . . .It's hard to keep that sense of urgency going the longer you run your project."

The American Revolution
raised $114,419 in 30 days

Bill Lichtenstein, who created this campaign to raise funds to make a documentary about pioneering Boston rock-radio station WBCN, explains: "If you look at almost any account of anybody who's done one of these things, usually they'll say, *Don't do more than thirty days. It will kill you. Or plan to take a two-week vacation afterward. It's exhausting.* I thought: *How exhausting can it be? It's like eBay!* But it's not."

Crania Anatomica Filigre
raised $77,271 in 45 days

Joshua Harker, the sculptor behind this project to produce ornate, 3D-printed skulls, explains his campaign's duration: "I ran my campaign for forty-five days. I think a project can lose steam if overextended, but in my opinion it seems that advice is more for time-sensitive event-type projects or fund-raising. My project happened to be more of an experiment/exploration of the viability of using crowdfunding to introduce and share art, as well as to sell it. I think I could've easily hit the $100,000 mark had I gone another couple weeks. That said, the management of the campaign became surprisingly overwhelming and consuming. I was happy for what it achieved, but glad when it was over."

Freaker USA: Making You And Your Beverage Cooler!
raised $62,770 in 60 days

Explains Freaker creator Zach Crain: "We were under the impression that a sixty-day campaign was the most commonly used time frame. We didn't want to rush anything with thirty days. Sixty felt right. It gave us time to do a couple promotional parties and really get the word out there while still being able to stay focused, work hard, and know that procrastination was not an option."

6.

LIGHTS, CAMERA, ACTION

Making the All-Important Kickstarter Video

I N 2009, ABOUT HALF of all Kickstarter projects launched with a video. In 2011, that number had risen to 80 percent, and today a successful campaign without a video that tells its story is a rare and special case. "Backers love pressing Play," says Kickstarter's official blog.

A successful Kickstarter video needs to get potential backers excited not only about your film/music/gadget but also about you. If you want people to take the not-so-small step of giving you their money, then you need to convince them that you are passionate about the project and capable of delivering on your promises. People want to see your face. They want to see your product (doing what it's supposed to do, if possible). They want to hear how well you sing or dance or play an instrument.

"To me, the video is key," says Nano Whitman, who raised $15,950 to finish an album and take his band on tour. "Whatever you write and all those gifts are secondary. It's the video that makes people feel like they want to give something to you or not."

What makes a successful Kickstarter video? How long should it be? What information needs to be included? Must you appear in your own video? (Mostly people do, since backers like to meet the makers.) Does it need to be done with professional equipment? (No.

Some successful Kickstarter videos have been shot with a phone or laptop webcams. Kickstarter supports direct upload of video in almost every digital format: MOV, MPEG, AVI, MP4, 3GP, WMV, and FLP up to 250 MB.)

It may come as no surprise that the most funded category on Kickstarter is Film and Video. Filmmakers and videographers have an obvious advantage and usually make exceptional videos that work to sway viewers. After all, that's what they're trained to do. A filmmaker will often show a trailer for a movie that needs funds for further production. That's what Boston filmmaker Bill Lichtenstein did to raise $114,419 to make a documentary about the radio station WBCN. He didn't appear in the video—it's a raucous collage of old footage and stills and interviews. As he explains: "The sense was that the usual kind of Kickstarter approach didn't quite fit, the *Hi, I've got this wild dream—dreams are free, but to make things happen you need money.* Jennifer Fox had just raised $150,000 for her documentary [**My Reincarnation**] and didn't appear in the video. She just said, *this is the work.*"

Other Kickstarter campaigners have chosen to appear onscreen themselves, and doing so can help boost a project a lot. Some people who are camera-shy have found that it helps to have another person—a friend, a cocreator, anyone—in the shot, too.

This may sound cynical, but in Kickstarter as in the rest of life, appearances matter. Time after time, when videos feature pretty women and/or cool guys who are passionate about their projects, the funding seems to go pretty well. This observation is purely nonscientific, based only on the viewing of a lot of Kickstarter videos. But it's a fact of life: attractiveness can attract things. Yes, you do need a compelling project. And you need to assure backers that you can get the work done. But the cool guy/cute girl factor is no less prevalent on Kickstarter than it is in any other part of life. Some of the examples in this chapter offer evidence to support this fact.

There are no rules to making a compelling Kickstarter video. There are only guidelines and good tips. The best thing you can do is to watch a lot of videos that have worked. They're the best source of ideas that might work for you. Here is a gallery of images from successful Kickstarter videos along with explanations about them by their creators.

Nano Whitman - an album, a tour

video length: 2:43
campaign sought: $11,000
campaign raised: $15,950

Open with a tight shot of musician Nano Whitman's face. He says:

  "Hey, what's happenin'? I'm Nano. It's a beautiful rainy day in Austin, Texas, and I'm glad you're here, because I'm trying to take my band on tour, and I'm trying to finish my album. So instead of doing something fancy for my Kickstarter video, I wrote a song for you."

The camera pulls back to show him with an acoustic guitar, sitting in the back of his van. Then he strums and sings his pitch. The chorus goes: "*Whoa-oa, start me up and be my Kickstarter / I thank you now for every dime, every dollar / and every little way that you always have helped me grow / Won't you kick-start my heart and get my band on the road?*"

Whitman explains his approach: "My music is often about saying something uncomfortable. When you do it in a song, it's OK, it's approachable. It doesn't make people feel ill at ease. So there I was, I was totally uncomfortable, thinking, *I'm not gonna be able to pull off looking in a camera and saying, 'give me money.'* But I could totally sing it, if I sort of couch it in my style of lyrics. And when I realized, *oh, I can sing my request to people?* I was OK with it.

"You want to think about who is gonna give you the money. If it's your parents' friends, they're interested in something professional. They're used to watching TV and movies. In my video the look is simple and clean, the sound is nice, and I felt like that was my audience. I felt that those are the people who were going to give more money. We purposefully made it as simple as possible and just featured the song." Looking back, he now jokes that the video is "impossibly cheesy."

Whitman explains that the video was technically just two shots, so it needed very little editing. It was indeed raining, so they moved the van under a canopy. "A friend of mine who's a filmmaker did direct and produce the video as his contribution to my campaign," Whitman says. They used an HD camera and a boom mic and didn't use a sound board. The video worked: "I woke up the next morning and I had already raised, like, $3,000. It just took off," he says. He thought maybe the folks at Kickstarter headquarters would like his Kickstarter song enough that they'd endorse or adopt it. That hasn't happened yet.

Pen Type-A: A minimal pen

video length: 3:15
campaign sought: $25,000
campaign raised: $281,989

Chei-Wei Wang and Taylor Levy, two product designers based in Brooklyn, did their entire video in split-screen, with two things happening at once. When you see how much money they raised, well, obviously, it worked.

On the left-hand side, the two of them casually describe their project. A silent demonstration of their product—a durable stainless steel holder for a common plastic pen—runs on the right. The split-screen was an inexpensive and easy way to keep the video visually interesting. It minimizes the amount of editing they had to do—no need to cut back and forth between them and the product demo. The video was put together using Final Cut software on a Mac. The close-ups of the pen were shot using a fancy digital camera that their design studio owned, but the video of the two designers talking was shot using a laptop webcam.

"We are both pretty shy and don't like being in front of the camera," Levy says. "Our first round was actually us drawing only, and we wanted to maybe talk over us drawing. We spent about a day shooting that, and we realized that it just didn't look good. It wasn't engaging. So we had to kind of bite the bullet. What you see in the video was our first take, actually. We did a bunch after that. But they were too rehearsed."

RIOT—L.A.'s Alternative Comedy Festival

video length: 2:16
campaign sought: $20,000
campaign raised: $22,380

Got celebrities? They can help a lot. Abbey Londer produces stand-up comedy shows in Los Angeles in hip venues like warehouses and Chinese restaurants, and she's worked with many of the comedians who perform in the area. When she got the idea to launch a new comedy festival in the city, she was able to persuade dozens of comedians (including Patton Oswalt and Bob Odenkirk) to come to a studio for free to shoot this goofy black-and-white video, a parody of a desperate plea to help a dire cause. Each comedian said only a sentence fragment. It took five total to say: "Every other second, 847 people don't laugh. Ninety percent of the world's laughter is owned by one percent of the world's population. The problem is ginormous."

"We have just over forty comedians in the video," Londer says. "Basically, I've submerged myself in the comedy scene in L.A. for the last three years and have been fortunate enough to meet and work with and produce shows with many of the comedians in the video. In addition, I got super lucky because *Funny or Die* let us use their new studio to shoot in—and comedians get a little more excited about a project when their name is affiliated in any way. It's not an *FOD*-branded video, just to make that clear. Once names started being attached to the project, more and more jumped in." The video quickly went viral, first on comedy websites and then beyond. Many of the comedians who participated in the video tweeted links to their many followers—another benefit of associating a project with well-known people. Londer also filmed extra of the comics of ad-libbing material that was edited into videos used as updates and bonuses during the campaign, which also set up its own YouTube channel.

Elevation Dock: The Best Dock for iPhone

video length: 2:45
campaign sought: $75,000
campaign raised: $1,464,706

Here's an A+ video that does exactly what it needs to do. It presents a great idea that solves a real problem, and it helps viewers (aka potential backers) clearly understand that something new has come along. First, we get a funny montage of existing tabletop iPhone docks, all working horribly. They're flimsy and plastic, they wobble. They're hard to remove from a phone even when you shake the device rather violently. After twenty-seven seconds of frustration with those products, the silly music in the background switches to a grandiose version of Pachelbel's Canon, and we see a soaring glamour shot of a much more solid looking metal dock. The camera circles it admiringly.

Next, our project creator comes on: *"Hey Kickstarter, my name's Casey. If you've tried to use docks for your iPhone, you've probably been as frustrated as I have."* Great opening line. No nonsense. Then we see that the product is real and that it works. Maybe the best shot in the video shows a chunk of metal for the new dock being machine tooled. It's visual proof that the product is real and money has been spent to produce it.

Freaker USA—Making You and Your Beverage Cooler

video length: 5:32
campaign sought: $48,500
campaign raised: $62,770

The video for the Freaker is a tour-de-force in marketing, even though Zach Crain, the main man behind the project, claims to have no marketing training and not a lot of formal education. This video has done the improbable: it made knit socks that you put around bottles and cans to minimize moisture (they're sometimes called coozies) seem unbelievably cool. The video is hosted by Crain, who comes off as an adorable, upbeat, hillbilly, stoner-type character, which doesn't seem far from reality when you talk with him.

"That was actually the first time I've ever been on camera," he says. The video was directed and shot by Oliver Mellan, a member of the Freaker team with formal training in film. It's not a short video, clocking in at nearly six minutes. It begins with Crain going completely off-topic, complimenting the viewer's shoes and hair and smell. He seems like a nice guy. Then it shows the problem that the Freaker is designed to remedy: all the lousy drink holders that are bulky, inconvenient, ineffective. Now here's the Freaker, which is soft and one size fits all. There's a slightly erotic series of demonstrations. Then a rapid-fire backstory about Crain's time living in a car, zigzagging around the country, working in a coffee shop, and attending a "Stitch & Bitch" knitting club, where he didn't want to make a scarf, so he made a beer coozy instead. He made more coozies, ate pancakes. The Freaker team got started. The video shows Lauren Krakauskas, a team member who does social media marketing (the cool guy/cute girl factor is clearly at work here). Then it's back to Zach for more fun ad-libs, a quiet refrigerator-door pitch for money, and a final graphic with all the details about how to pledge. The project was massively successful and won 2,416 backers.

Yet even with that last panel with details about how to pledge, the video left some viewers confused. "Our video got out there pretty fast and started moving around," Crain says. "The biggest problem we had with it was that people would share it on Facebook, and people would watch it, but they wouldn't know what Kickstarter was. So then they'd just be like, *OK, that was a really cute video.*"

Kickstarter Video Tips

Here are half a dozen ways to make your campaign pitch stand a chance at success.

1. **Get to the point.** When you include a video, potential backers may not take the time to read your written pitch, so within twenty to thirty seconds you should let them know exactly what you're trying to accomplish. Got a product? What problem does it solve? What new power does it give its users? Got a movie or book—what is it about?

2. **Show as much as you can.** A physical prototype is better than a computer model. A functional prototype is even better. A finished product that viewers can imagine using right then and there is best. A scene from a movie is better than an idea for a movie. Some special dice or tokens for a game are better than mock-up drawings of yet-to-be-realized items. A book you want to make from your years of webcomics or blogging is more real than a book you just have an idea about writing.

3. **Draft a friend.** If you're camera shy, it really does help if you appear onscreen with someone else, someone with whom you have a good rapport. Your camaraderie and shared enthusiasm for the project can loosen things up, and that relaxed confidence looks good to potential backers.

4. **Avoid using copyrighted material.** "Borrowing," "sampling," whatever you want to call it—using art, videos, images, songs, and the like that you haven't created yourself and don't own is almost always illegal, and in a community

of creative artists where originality is valued, blatantly using another person's work will send a negative message. Legal and free or low-cost sources of audio and video content are available on the Web. For soundtrack music, try SoundCloud, the Vimeo Music Store, Free Music Archive, and ccMixter. The Prelinger Archive is one resource at Archive.org that offers free-to-use video clips.

5. **Take the time to get it right.** This is your public face. Reshoot and take the time in the editing phase to show you care. Little glitches matter. Redo the sound if you need to. Potential backers may judge the effort you put into the video as an indication of the effort you'll put into the project.

6. **Don't forget to say how to donate.** Be sure to include text at the end of the video that explicitly identifies it as part of your Kickstarter campaign, including the URLs for the Kickstarter page as well as for your own website (if you have one). Good videos do go viral and may be embedded elsewhere. The last thing you want is for someone to love your video but not know exactly how to donate—or not even realize it's connected to a fund-raising campaign.

7.

THE KICKOFF!

Building your project and launching it

ONCE YOU'VE FIGURED OUT all the critical details, it's time to build your project at Kickstarter.com. Click the Start link at the top of Kickstarter's home page, and you're off to the races.

Kickstarter has streamlined the process of initiating a campaign. In the olden days (prior to early 2012), users needed to submit a short proposal explaining what they were planning and then wait for it to be approved; upon approval, they could then build the page that describes the project to the public and solicits pledges. Now, you just build a campaign page right away. It functions as your proposal, and once approved by Kickstarter it is ready to release into the wild. The process goes like this:

1. Build a project.
2. Submit it for approval by Kickstarter's Community Team.
3. The project exists initially as a private "preview link," which resembles a real project page but cannot accept pledges. It's not public and is accessible only to those with whom you share the URL. You can get feedback from trusted advisors at this stage and tweak the content as necessary.
4. The project is approved (or rejected) within a couple of days.
5. If approved, launch.

Building the Project

Kickstarter's Web interface makes building a project so simple, it almost doesn't need to be explained. You'll click through introductory screens reminding you of the guidelines and eligibility requirements (covered in chapter 1, "Before You Start"). Kickstarter will provide a link to their useful "Kickstarter School," which is a good accompaniment to the information in this book. Then you'll arrive at a series of forms to fill out where you will input your project. Now it's getting exciting. Here we go!

The Basics

In this section, you will provide the project's title and category, your location, a short blurb about the project (135 characters maximum), the campaign's duration (a set number of days or a specific end date), your fund-raising goal, and an image to represent the project in the baseball-card-like widget for it that will appear on Kickstarter. A sample widget will display and populate itself with the information and image you provide. Hit Save when you're ready. You can go back and change this information later, if needed.

Rewards: Enter the rewards you've decided on here. See chapter 2, "Pledges and Rewards," for explanations and worksheets to help you figure out this crucial part of your campaign.

Story: Here's where you enter the main text describing your project. This text supplements your video, but it's best to approach it as though there is no accompanying video—you should describe your project completely and compellingly. Make sure to explain near the beginning exactly what your project is. You can include details that aren't in your video, maybe a breakdown of how you plan to use the funding, or images that show the evolution of your product's design, or pictures from your previous artwork or performances. This is your written pitch, so make the most of it. You can include links, images, and additional embedded videos as well. The story section can be updated at any time during a Kickstarter campaign.

About You: A bit of biographical information, including a photo and your website(s). Your photo will go on top of your Kickstarter member page, where all the projects that you've either launched or backed will be listed.

Account: Kickstarter wants to have your active e-mail address and phone number. Once you type those here, Kickstarter will auto-call and e-mail you to confirm that the contact information is accurate.

You'll also need to establish an Amazon Payments account, which will be the mechanism by which you'll receive your funding, if you succeed. You must take care of this step now, even before your project is accepted and you receive any funds, and it could take a day or more to establish and verify the account. This separate process is performed at the payments.amazon.com website.

You can add Amazon Payments capability to an existing Amazon account or start a new account specifically for it. In either case, you must use the same e-mail address as the one you've supplied on Kickstarter for your Amazon Payments account. Amazon Payments requires you to set up a link to a U.S. bank account. They'll ask for your bank's routing number and your account number, and, to confirm that you control the account, they will either ask you for your online-banking user ID and password (for instant confirmation) or make two tiny, random deposits into the account, whose amounts you will need to note and accurately report back to Amazon. The deposits take a day or so to be disbursed; if you're not participating in online banking, you'll have to find out about them the old-fashioned way, by checking with a teller (in person or by phone) or looking at your printed statement. It goes without saying that you should follow all the careful security and privacy measures you normally take whenever you share any financial information online. You may not want to give Amazon Payments your banking password and might feel more comfortable using the slower method of verifying the deposits (plus, it's a fun way to receive several free cents). Once Amazon Payments verifies your account, Kickstarter lets you move on to review all the information you've keyed in and to submit your project for approval. If you're ready to roll, do it.

Preview Link: Once you submit the project, you get to see a preview version of your campaign page. You also get a link for it—a URL that you can share with anyone you'd like, post on Facebook, share on Twitter, however you want to get it to people for review. You won't be able to accept pledges yet, but you can let people know your project is coming and show them exactly what it will look like. This prelaunch phase is a good time to collect feedback. You're able to tweak any aspect of the project, including rewards descriptions and pledge levels, your story, and your video. Within a couple of days you'll know if Kickstarter has approved your project. If they do, you'll get a message saying something like this:

All systems go! We've reviewed your project and it looks like everything falls within our guidelines. Hooray! This means that whenever you're ready, you can hit the green launch button and make your project live. There's no deadline to launch, though, so take your time.

Remember to keep our guidelines in mind if you're making any changes. We take our guidelines pretty seriously and ask our community to keep an eye out for them, too. When we find things that are objectionable, whether we missed them during our review or they were added after the fact, we remove projects from our site's browse functionality until they're fixed. In extreme cases, we remove the project altogether. That's unpleasant for everyone, so just be sure everything's within code before you launch! You'll do great! We can't wait to see your project live.

You'll also get some final guidelines, including a reminder of the fees that Kickstarter and Amazon will take at the end of a successful campaign, a reminder that a project can never be deleted or modified (except for updates), and a warning that "if you fundamentally change your project, are unable to fulfill the promises made to backers, or decide to abandon the project for any reason, you are expected to cancel your project. A failure to do so could result in damage to your reputation or even legal action on behalf of your backers." But that ain't gonna happen, right?

Launch! So you've launched your Kickstarter campaign. Get ready to work! The funding of your creative dream is officially on the clock. It's win or go home. The days begin counting down. The funds begin adding up. Now what?

Kickstarter campaign tools

As soon as you launch your project, your page will change from "preview" status to "live." You're ready to receive real pledges. Anyone on the Web or on Kickstarter will be able to find your project page, and within minutes it may even start coming up in Google searches.

If you're logged in as a campaign creator, near the top of your project page you'll see four tools to work with. One of them you've seen before, but the other three are new:

1. Edit project

This tool is familiar. Here, you can click through the same set of screens as the ones you used to set up your campaign. You can modify anything on your project page—including its title—*except* the description and pledge amount for a reward that a backer has already chosen. (There is one change you can make to a reward that's already been chosen. You can set a limit on how many of that reward are available, as long as it's not lower than the number of people who have already chosen that reward.) You also can add new rewards, images, links, and information to the project description, and you can add or append a project FAQ.

2. Dashboard

Like the dashboard in a car, this is where you see how fast you're going and how far you've gone. You're going to look at this page a lot during your fund drive.

The first dashboard graphic is the **Funding Progress** chart, a graph that shows how much has been pledged, day by day, in a dollar amount and in a percentage of your goal. These graphs follow different patterns depending on the campaign. For many campaigns they rocket up at the very beginning, surging quickly past the goal line. Some start with a small spurt as early backers jump in, then level off, then climb again as the final days approach. Others never get much lift at all.

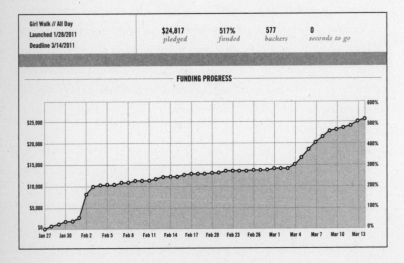

Jacob Krupnick, a New York filmmaker behind a 45-day campaign to raise funds to make the film **Girl Walk // All Day**, has kindly shared his progress chart. It shows a common funding pattern, with an early thrust, then a plateau in the middle period, and a steady finishing kick.

"We had two major spikes in the campaign," Krupnick says. "In the beginning, like most people who run a good game with their social networks, we did decently right out of the gate. We had a bunch of people who were donating small amounts, and I think by the end of the first day we were close to $800 or $1,000 from probably fifty or sixty people, which felt great. It was friends and family and the immediate people inspired by the project. On day six [February 1—check out the spike in the chart], Kickstarter publicized the project in their newsletter as one of their three favorites. That day we crossed our finish line, which was set at $4,800. We had close to $6,000 or $7,000.

"Then it tapered off. It was steady for a month or so. I'd been having a running conversation with someone at the *New York Times Magazine*. That article came out [March 4—check out the chart] and we had a four or five thousand dollar spike in the last few days."

Also on the dashboard is a bar chart showing the popularity of each of your reward levels. Keep an eye on this section—if your campaign is a success, it ends up being a picture of your commitment to backers. If a reward has no takers yet, there's still time to change its description and pledge amount or delete it altogether.

If a reward seems to be getting too popular—nearing a level higher than you can deliver—you can go in and impose a limit to the number available, as long as it's not lower than the amount you're already on the hook to deliver. Looking at the chart, you may see a price point at which it could be popular to add a new reward.

Finally, the dashboard has a list of all campaign activity, whether it's a pledge, an update, an adjustment, or a visitor comment.

3. Backer report

Here's where you will get a breakdown of backers by pledge amount and have the opportunity to send them all—or just those at selected levels—e-mail messages. It's also from this screen that, after a successful Kickstarter campaign, you'll send all the backers a survey asking for their shipping addresses, product preferences, and anything else you need to know to get them the rewards they pledged for.

4. Post Update

You can post updates as often as you'd like. They may contain text, links, images, and video. There's plenty of flexibility to be creative with updates, and they can be a solid way to keep the campaign's momentum alive. "I'd advise Kickstarter people to keep releasing as much new content as you can, to keep people interested," says comedy-show promoter Abbey Londer.

Your audience has access to updates from your main project page. Updates don't overwrite or supersede the main project description but instead are viewable by clicking a separate tab on the main page. Updates can be posted for anyone to see or for backers' eyes only. Either way, backers who have pledged to the campaign will receive an automatic e-mail when any update has been posted, so don't overdo it. Multiple daily updates can quickly get annoying, particularly to people who have pledged and may feel they've done their part and want to be left alone now, please.

Updates shouldn't be spam or filler. Ideally, they're informative, welcome little treats. The Kickstarter staff once likened good updates to "behind-the-scenes DVD features." They can be used to make backers feel happy and assured that they have put their pledge money into good hands. Maybe you've taken a big step in the creation of your artwork or music or product. Maybe you've received some super media coverage that you just have to crow about (perhaps making backers feel smart that they knew you before you were famous).

Updates can be entertaining new content. Comedy-show promoter Abbey Londer, who raised $22,380 in early 2012 to start **RIOT**, an indie comedy festival in Los Angeles, was fortunate enough to get more than forty comedians to participate in the main video for her campaign (check out more details about her video in chapter 6, "Lights, Camera, Action"). She also was smart enough to videotape extra footage of the comedians ad-libbing about the worst places they'd done comedy. She edited that material into multiple snippets, some of which were funnier than the original video, and she posted the extra videos 'as updates in Kickstarter and on a YouTube channel she set up for the campaign. Some of the update videos went a little bit viral themselves. They were indeed an extra treat, drawing continued attention to the campaign and keeping fans amused.

Chris Schlarb, who raised $2,399 to make a documentary about ice cream trucks called **We Scream: Voices From The Ice Cream Underground**, posted updates on his travels around the country meeting ice-cream truck drivers, and he added new video footage as he filmed it. For her project **Keep Music Indie**, April Smith, a New York musician, posted a midcampaign update just for backers offering a special incentive: if her project hit 50 percent of her $10,000 goal by a certain day, she promised to post a new song exclusively for them. She got the funding and posted a video of herself playing the new song. One of the pioneers in the art of Kickstarter updates has been musician Allison Weiss. For her first campaign, called **Allison Weiss makes a full-length record!** her updates included taking requests for a show, soliciting album title ideas and fan votes, and offering many video and text updates from her studio. In one update, she offered to do a phone call with the person whose pledge pushed her past her $2,000 goal (she ended up raising $7,711). She followed that with an update containing an entertaining video of the Skype call she made to Melbourne, Australia, to chat with the backer who made the victory-clinching pledge.

Updates can continue well after a campaign has been successful. After Weiss's first project ended in triumph in early August of 2009, she continued to send updates for another nine months, through December of that year. The last one she posted, update number 25, came on the heels of the *New York Times* mention of her in an article about Kickstarter success stories. She smartly made it one of her few updates that wasn't restricted to backers. It was aimed in part at people who saw the newspaper article but hadn't been part of her campaign originally. She posted her tour schedule and offered a way to buy her album to anyone who hadn't pledged! She wrote, in part: "By now, many of you have received your rewards and preorders promised to you for helping me make this dream a reality. If you still haven't gotten a copy, consider picking one up anywhere mp3's are sold (iTunes, Amazon, etc.) or getting a physical one straight from me at http://allisonw.com/store." Smart.

Filmmaker Lucas McNelly's Kickstarter project **A Year Without Rent** was set up to allow him to spend a year traveling the country, working on indie films. So it made sense that he had many updates after the campaign, with photos and videos showing projects he worked on all over the place. His campaign ended in January 2011, and he filed his final update more than a year later, in February 2012. That update began: "This is the update where I'm supposed to get all teary-eyed and profound." It ended: "Thank you, from the bottom of my heart. It's been a hell of a year."

Respond to comments, update the FAQ

Much of the Kickstarter ethos rests in the belief that your backers are going along with you on a journey as, together, we give birth to this wonderful new creation that might not come into existence without their help. Backers really do have a special, ground-floor connection to your project. You're captaining a team with a common goal. Keeping it feeling interactive and like a true community is a big part of that. Because the **Detroit Needs A Statue of Robocop** campaign was unique—as a local initiative that attracted backers from far beyond the Michigan city—the creators felt a special need to keep everyone invested in the project, even if they weren't local.

"Engaging the backers is a big thing. We spent a lot of time with that," says campaign member Brandon Walley. "We framed it to them that they're co-owners of the RoboCop statue, making constant updates and keeping them happy. They're part of this, they're along for this journey. Someone in Sweden who's willing to donate $100 doesn't really care about the RoboCop statue in Detroit—but it's the idea that he was part of something really cool and different, and he got this cool RoboCop Detroit T-shirt, and we were constantly sending updates. We have a really active Facebook page, and backers are on there. From what I see from unsuccessful Kickstarters, that's usually one of the indicators. If people approach it like, *Oh, I'm an artist and help me do this*, it's not gonna be as successful as: *Come on this journey with me*."

Besides being active with updates, you'll want to be online responding to comments people post on your project page on the very day they come in. And you should update your FAQ liberally whenever you feel there are unanswered questions about your project or its aims.

"You get this extraordinary instant feedback from people during a campaign," says filmmaker Bill Lichtenstein. He had been using the canned trailer for his planned documentary **The American Revolution** as his Kickstarter video, but midway through the campaign he had received enough advice that his team decided to recut the trailer for Kickstarter, making it clearer what the film was about.

Grinding through a campaign

Speaking with someone who is in the middle of a Kickstarter campaign can be a little like talking to a crazy person. They often are frazzled, distracted, overwhelmed. "It's a little bit scary," Pete Taylor said two days after the launch of his **SAVORx** campaign. He had raised only $175, barely more than 1 percent of his goal. "Say if I get one hundred bucks a day now, I'll make it—no, I won't," he said, correcting himself. "Hold on, I gotta do the math. Like I say, I haven't slept. I cannot express how nerve-wracking—I think I'm gonna have a heart attack. I just spent two months of my life perfecting this pitch, for my dream. I think we're gonna hit it, though. I really think that."

Challenges may arise completely out of the blue during a campaign. The Detroit RoboCop statute project in March 2011 ended up encountering unanticipated resistance in the real-life, offline world. The city of Detroit had mixed feelings about the project. Detroit Mayor Dave Bing (yes, the former NBA basketball player) publicly said that a statue of RoboCop was not on his agenda. Residents of some communities were put off by the idea of honoring a robotic law-enforcement-machine.

"We were going to community meetings where people were standing up in outrage, yelling and screaming at us: *You can't put this in our neighborhood*," says Brandon Walley, one of the partners behind the RoboCop statue campaign. "Some people felt insulted. I heard a lot of crazy things—that it was an oppressive image. It's not the right representation. To me, that wasn't a really thought-out stance. But we would listen to them and explain what our motives were."

Zach Crain of the **Freaker** team says that their 60-day campaign experienced "a nice little start, and then there was a big, really slow period. I think we had only, like, $13,000 [of a $48,500 goal] with two weeks left to go, so the pressure was on! Everybody was getting a little nervous. But it pushed us to keep pushing it. We kept doing videos in the slower time, to keep providing for the people who had already donated or were coming on. I was always really confident that it was going to work out. Definitely just keep moving, keep going forward."

8.

BUILD THE BUZZ

How to get attention for your campaign
via the media and social networks

THE MEDIA CAN PLAY a gigantic role in a Kickstarter campaign. It's really an X factor and often, to uncork another cliché, a game-changer. One minute you're struggling to get even your dear friends to pay attention to your campaign. The next moment a blogger proclaims that your project is groovier than Greg Brady, and you're getting thousands of people from all over the world taking a look, maybe hundreds of pledges, maybe tens of thousands of dollars. It can happen fast, and it can snowball when still more blogs, always hungry for news and links, pick up an original post about your campaign and reblog it, passing the buzz along to an even wider audience.

"We sent a note to the Pen Addict blog. Then we sent an e-mail to the blog Swissmiss. It just exploded after that," says Taylor Levy, who, with partner Chei-Wei Wang, raised $281,989 in August 2011 for **Pen Type-A**, a stylish pen holder. "The spike from Swissmiss was like 600 people a day for two days."

The press played a big role for Scott Thrift and his elegant one-year clock, **The Present**. "It got press pretty quickly, because it's such a strange idea, and fun to talk about, and fun to think about the season and time," he says. "There was a *Fast Company* article that was pretty elaborate. They had written a couple of other articles about us, and I had built a relationship with them. The *Fast Company* story came out the day after we launched. That hit, then the next day *Creativity* magazine. It's been in a lot of publications all over the world since then."

The media attention you'll get during a Kickstarter campaign is unpredictable. What will excite any given member of the media is impossible to know in advance. This chapter relates the experiences of many Kickstarter campaigners, offers advice from bloggers who have covered Kickstarter campaigns, and includes lots of other tips and tools to take some of the guesswork out of the wondrous world of media relations.

Plan for the future

Despite the difficulty in predicting how (or if) the media will respond to your Kickstarter effort, you ought to have in place a media plan before launching your campaign. Compiling a list of media outlets and bloggers that you'll reach out to is a solid start. You'll want to begin assembling this contact list before your launch so that, when your campaign does go live, you can send immediate alerts to targeted media, announcing your arrival while the news is still fresh. No news outlet likes to be late to a story, and they like it even better when they can be the first to tell readers that something truly awesome is about to break. Kickstarter's all-or-nothing deadline system provides a built-in story of struggle that you can relate to the media, too, and the approach of your deadline toward the final days of a campaign can be another moment of media interest, a selling point for your story.

"In a month you're able to generate a large amount of PR heat," says filmmaker Bill Lichtenstein, who raised $114,419 for **The American Revolution**, his documentary about a pioneering Boston rock-radio station whose frequency was 104 on the FM dial. "Suddenly, if you call the newspaper and say, *We're trying to raise $104,000*, it becomes a news story."

Though no one has measured it scientifically, media coverage of individual Kickstarter campaigns likely tends to follow the same U-shaped pattern as for pledges: peaking at the start and the finish, with a lull in the middle. (See the graph on page 88.)

Of course, we all have our own media networks these days, right? You'll need to reach out to contacts through social networks, and today there are more tools than ever for doing so. The goal isn't to repeatedly badger your close friends but to use the resources available to reach a broader audience. "It's all been through social networking for us. Facebook and Twitter," said Abbey Londer, creator of the **RIOT** comedy festival, during her January 2012 campaign. "We have a list of blogs that we haven't even tapped yet. Laughspin [a big comedy website] wrote us up on day one or day two. The video did go a little bit viral—Megan Mullally [a comedian in the Kickstarter video], her fan site posted it, and I think that brought in a lot of attention. All the comedians have been tweeting about it, which has been awesome."

Social media and traditional media can work in concert for you. A writer may notice a Facebook post about your project and write a story; the story then becomes a link that you can post on social networks. They call it a news cycle for a reason!

"I had lined up a couple things beforehand to announce the project launch," says Joshua Harker, whose **Crania Anatomica Filigre** campaign in October 2011 became Kickstarter's most-funded sculpture project (it raised $77,271). "I sent out a newsletter and the obligatory Twitter and Facebook stuff. Social networking was huge. I've got a fairly large following on Facebook and extensive contacts through LinkedIn that I tried to mine. I posted multiple times per day and submitted to blogs endlessly throughout the campaign. No spam, though. The vendors I used for my rewards got in on it and posted about the project and did inclusions in their newsletters as well. The project went viral about the third day and just went silly-time from there. There were articles, interviews, blogs, and repost after repost across the Internet. Success in anything, I suppose, is a perfect storm of chemistry, hard work, and timing. I tried diligently to do all I could to get myself centered in front of the train coming down the rail. After that, you just need the resources to help jump aboard—and not get run down!"

Leverage social media and other online tools

Here's a rundown of the major Web-based avenues to get your message out.

Build a website: Though your Kickstarter project page is central headquarters for your campaign, creating a separate website for your art/project/venture can add a lot of legitimacy to your effort. There are different approaches. Most artists, designers, writers, and entrepreneurs have already established websites, and at minimum you'll want to update your existing website to let people know about the fund-raising campaign. Kickstarter provides a useful tool: code that allows you to embed your Kickstarter widget (that little onscreen baseball card summarizing the project) and your project's video onto any website or blog. On every project page under the video there's an Embed button. Click that button to get the HTML code and then paste the widget or video onto a website or blog.

You might also set up a separate website just for your Kickstarter project. Comedy-festival organizer Abbey Londer has her own site for her comedy-booking business, but she established riotla.com for her effort to create the **RIOT** comedy festival. While she was raising funds on Kickstarter, she set up that URL to redirect to her Kickstarter page. After she met her goal, she turned off the redirect and began building content on the riotla.com site, adding video from the campaign and links to media coverage of her Kickstarter project. Eventually, riotla.com evolved into a resource for scheduling and other information about the fall 2012 festival.

Musician Allison Weiss used a bit of both approaches. She kept her own website but set up the address alisonw.com/donate to redirect to Kickstarter—it would automatically send visitors to her first, and, later, her second Kickstarter campaign.

Facebook: Facebook posts can highlight your latest Kickstarter updates and link to the media coverage your campaign has received. Just as with websites, it may make sense for you to establish a separate Facebook presence for your Kickstarter project. You'll certainly maintain your own personal Facebook page as a way to keep your friends posted on your Kickstarter campaign's progress (and you'll do plenty of that), but the people from around the country and the world who may want to receive Facebook updates about your project are a different set of people. It's a good idea to give these helpful strangers a way to "like" your Kickstarter project without forcing them to see photos of your nieces.

Facebook is more than just your own wall. If you have a food-related Kickstarter project, find foodie pages on Facebook and post to those walls to reach existing masses of potential backers who have congregated around their special interest. You'd be surprised how many results come up with a Google search for, say, "Facebook foodie pages." Some celebrities, local radio and TV stations, newspapers, subject-matter experts, associations, and clubs and special-interest groups allow anyone to post on their Facebook walls. Think about your audience and find out where *they* find out about stuff they think is cool.

Another possible way to use Facebook's reach is via ads, those little sponsored links that show up along the right-hand column of the screen. Yes, anyone can buy those. Maybe you just ignore them. But they are well-targeted, and apparently they do get clicked on. "They're relatively cheap to do," says Josh Hartung, a partner in the successful Kickstarter campaign for **Loomi** paper lamp kits. "We spent about $200 or $300 on those and got some click-throughs."

Twitter: Just as with Facebook, and for the same reason, you may want to set up a separate Twitter feed for your Kickstarter project. Followers who like your project may not much care that you spilled coffee on yourself in a taxi, so keep your personal Twitter feed separate. As with Facebook, people who connect with you via Twitter stay connected beyond the duration of your campaign, so they can be informed of future projects. One tool that's useful for publicizing a Kickstarter campaign via Twitter is the shortened URL made available for every project. It works like bit.ly and tinyurl but begins with http://kck.st. You can find the short URL for your (or any) Kickstarter campaign in small type underneath the project's video.

YouTube: If you're making more than one or two videos for your campaign, building a YouTube channel for your project can be a great idea. It's free. YouTube is part of the Google empire, so it requires you to set up a new Google user account, and that will give you a new Gmail address connected with your Kickstarter campaign, which isn't a bad thing to have (even though most of your messaging with Kickstarter backers will go through Kickstarter's own messaging system).

LinkedIn: LinkedIn is a network for people, not projects, so you won't be setting up a separate account for your Kickstarter campaign on this site. But your personal LinkedIn feed can be a way to let your professional connections know about your Kickstarter campaign, including links to media coverage you receive.

Reaching friends of friends

Keep in mind that Facebook, Twitter, LinkedIn, photo-sharing sites, and other social media aren't just about reaching that first level of your friends and connections. If you're working it hard, you're also asking those people to repost, retweet, and pass along your Kickstarter campaign information to their own networks of connections, thereby multiplying your reach exponentially. If you're asking your friends to pass along news of your campaign by reposting and retweeting your Kickstarter news, it's also a way to remind them about the campaign without explicitly asking them for money. The partners behind the March 2012 Kickstarter campaign for **The HuMn Wallet**, a minimalistic wallet that blocks radio-frequency identification signals, instituted a formal referral system to promote pass-alongs: "If you can help us spread the word and are able to pull in 2 people to back our project (at any level) we will give you a free aluminum HuMn Wallet in your choice of color (including strap color)," they promised. "To get credited for the referral, the backers you referred will need to mention you by name in the 'Comments' tab."

Working with the media

Though contacting people in your own social networks is essential, few things kick-start a Kickstarter campaign more reliably than a positive mention in a popular blog or prominent news outlet. Many people who undertake Kickstarter campaigns have experience working with the media. Many work in the media. For others, "media relations" is an all-new experience and can be daunting. How does some random person go about getting mentioned in a blog? How do you get in touch with the local newspaper or with TV news people? How does it all work?

Of course, there's a whole industry devoted to getting good media coverage: the public-relations business. Some ambitious Kickstarter creators have gone so far as to hire PR agencies to help them get press for their campaigns, though that's not always a great idea. First of all, it can cost big bucks (it's better to have a PR-savvy friend help as a contribution to the project). Having an agency out there pushing your project can also run a little counter to Kickstarter's I-did-this-myself ethic. "I've heard some blowback about people hiring professional PR firms for their Kickstarters," says Matt Haughey, an Internet entrepreneur who has backed many Kickstarter projects. It may be hard to present yourself to the press as a struggling artist or underdog if you have a publicist.

Besides, you can do it yourself. To help you, we've interviewed several Kickstarter creators who talk about their strategies and experiences getting press. We've also talked to other people who spread the buzz: a professional publicist and some bloggers who cover Kickstarter campaigns. What turns them on? How should (and shouldn't) you approach them? Here's what to think about.

What's your story?

The media is in the business of telling stories, whether those stories are news items, upbeat features about compelling individuals, investigative pieces, or fun roundups of the latest gizmos. Nathaniel Hansen, a filmmaker, is in the business of telling stories, so he knows what he's talking about. After being involved in more than a dozen Kickstarter projects that together raised close to $350,000, he blogged some advice about how best to approach the media. He suggests that, before launching a Kickstarter campaign, you should consider crafting a story "treatment" that explains your saga and why it is a compelling tale, the way writers do for movies or novels. The story of your project becomes a useful narrative not just for getting media attention but for attracting backers as well.

"Feature film treatments that get shopped around might be sixty pages long," Hansen wrote. "Does your pitch need to be this complex? That depends on your personality and what you're trying to accomplish."

Realistically, sixty pages is probably overkill to explain the rationale behind a Kickstarter project. But Hansen is right in saying that you need to explain yourself: why should people care about what you're doing? Just the fact that your campaign exists isn't a story. The mere fact that you are using Kickstarter may have been novel and newsworthy to a journalist in 2010 or even in 2011, but "Area Man Uses Kickstarter" is not the stop-the-presses story it used to be. *We've already done a Kickstarter story*, a reporter will likely reply. *What's new about yours? What's compelling?*

Are you a struggling artist who was living on the streets and now is in the process of raising thousands of dollars? Are you honoring a cherished or forgotten local institution with your effort to create a film or book (or statue) about it? Everyone has stories. Figure out yours.

Who are your people?

After tapping your friends and family, and then your online friends and followers, you will need to reach out to the communities of shared interest that are likely to support your project. Some of these communities you may already be part of; others you will need to find. Aurora Guerrero is a filmmaker who used Kickstarter to raise money to finish making *Mosquita y Mari*, a quiet dramatic feature film about two Latina girls who have a romantic relationship. She reached out to the LGBT community and its media outlets. She reached out to Latino cultural organizations and their websites and newsletters. She reached out to the independent filmmaker community. All of these groups pitched in as she neared her fund-raising goal.

Identify your media

Once you have a good idea of who your audience is, the task is to get news about your campaign into the media outlets that your audience consumes for information. Are you making a folk-music album on which every song is an ode to bacon? Find the blogs, websites, and Facebook pages for bacon lovers and folk music. A documentary film about a boxer from inner-city Baltimore? Check into indie film sites, boxing sites, Baltimore news outlets. There's plenty of media to choose from: TV stations, radio stations, daily newspapers, weekly alternative papers, blogs affiliated with print magazines, blogs created by passionate individuals.

"A big part was to identify our market," says Josh Hartung about the **Loomi** paper-lamp-kit campaign. "We did the standard in terms of publicity, which is to cold e-mail a whole bunch of blogs. We sent out a lot of cold e-mails and at first got a lot of nothing back. We started out with the design market, but we found that wasn't super effective for us to target. We kept trying to get around the idea that people who are into design don't necessarily want to build their own lamps. We kept trying to hide it—*it's really easy to build!* What we discovered is that crafty people and DIY-design people were really into the idea that you build it. *They* think it's really cool. Once we identified that those are the people who wanted the product—which was something the Kickstarter campaign really helped us do—then we were able to target blogs in the crafts space, which were a much better fit. We were on Futuregirl and a few other blogs. A blog called Colossal [thisiscolossal.com] was huge for us, generating maybe $5,000 in funding."

Wes Garrett of the Park City, Utah, design firm Swarm, which ran two Kickstarter campaigns to fund the **Nectar and Elixir** bicycle accessories, says, "We had a long list of bicycle blogs that took us a long time to develop. We did a lot of posting to people's Facebook pages and walls. Any time we would get something posted on somebody's website or blog, we would then submit that to the curated news sites. The break was the blog Boing Boing. They did a post about us [on April 8, on a project that ended April 16], and on that day our traffic more than doubled. Once we got on Boing Boing it just went viral; tons of people posted it. I think we were on ten different blogs and Web pages a day. We were in the *Wall Street Journal*. It's kind of funny. We didn't know who the contact within Boing Boing was, and we sent a bunch of e-mails, repeated e-mails, over and over. There was at least one gentleman who had an affinity for the product. I think we got lucky that way."

At the risk of becoming out-of-date as the years go by—but with the reward of being helpful right away—a list of some of the online media outlets that have been friendly to Kickstarter projects, circa 2012, appears on pages 132–33. It's easy to update this list for yourself. Click over to these sites and search for "Kickstarter." See if they're still covering Kickstarter projects, how recently, and which writers' bylines are on the reports (those are the writers you may want to contact).

Also, look at recent Kickstarter projects that seem similar to yours and see where they are getting media coverage. If they're not listing their coverage prominently (they ought to be), you can Google their names. For example, type "Kickstarter Elevation Dock" or "Kickstarter Pebble" into Google, and you'll get links to dozens of websites and blogs that covered those wildly successful gadgets. Make sure to note whether a publication is covering the product (as in, "here's something really cool that readers might desire") or the business story (as in, "another Kickstarter campaign breaks a record"). In the latter case, they may not be interested in your campaign unless it brings some new wrinkle to the crowdfunding phenomenon.

Keep in mind that these sites may have other outlets for letting people know about your project, aside from their editorial coverage. Many sell small ads that could be appropriate for a Kickstarter campaign. They may also have discussion forums, where you can try to get people excited about your project by posting information and a link. In addition, some of these publications may hold events that you might attend or participate in. For example, if the timing is right and you're trying to get funding for a cool tabletop game, maybe you can share your idea with an audience of hardcore gamers at the annual Board Game Geek Con. You get the idea.

Kickstarter-Friendly Online Media

Ars Technica (technology, video games)

Autoblog (automotive)

Bicycling (bicycling)

BoardGameGeek (games)

Board Game Info (games)

Boing Boing (tech, pop culture, odd news)

Business Insider (tech business, gear)

Colossal (art and design)

Comics Alliance (comics)

Complex (gear, games, pop culture)

Designboom (design)

Design Sponge (design)

The Dice Tower (board games)

Engadget (gadgets)

Escapist (games)

Fast Company/FastCoDesign (business ideas, design, gadgets)

Film Courage (indie film)

Film Independent (indie film)

Film Threat (films; has also begun selling $50 "crowdfunding classifieds" ads)

Filmmaker (films; curates a Kickstarter page)

Flavorwire (music, film, culture)

Futuregirl (crafts, DIY apparel)

GearHungry ("stuff you'll want")

GeekDad (parenting)

Geekosystem (all things geeky)

GigaOM (tech/business)

Gizmodo (gadgets)

Gothamist (New York happenings; there's also Chicagoist, SFist, LAist, Austinist)

Inc.com (small-business stories, ideas)

Indiewire (indie film)

Inhabitant (eco-friendly design)

io9 (science/sci-fi)

Jalopnik (automotive)

Joystiq (video games)

Kill Screen (video games; promotes a "Kickstarter of the Day")

Kotaku (video games)

Laughing Squid (trends, gadgets, odd news)

Laughspin (comedy)

Lifehacker (gadgets, design, housewares)

MAKE (DIY projects)

Mashable (gadgets, tech business)

Mediabistro/Galleycat (publishing projects)

Neatorama (neat stuff)

Nerdist (comedy, pop culture)

PaidContent (publishing, media)

Paste (music)

Pitchfork (music; curates a Kickstarter page)

PSFK (design, fashion)

Purple Pawn (tabletop games)

SlashGear (gadgets, tech)

Swissmiss (cool designs and ideas)

TechCrunch (tech gear/business)

The Classical (sports)

The Verge (tech gear/business)

Twitch Film (indie movies)

Uncrate ("the digital magazine for guys who love stuff")

Wired/GadgetLab (new concepts, design, gadgets)

Can publicity stunts help?

The answer is yes, but not always. A grizzled newspaper journalist or hip website editor may see through an obvious gimmick that isn't focused on the quality of your product or project. On the other hand, a local TV station looking for timely, offbeat, visual stories may embrace a zany, attention-begging component of your Kickstarter campaign, and that could be its way of explaining the Kickstarter phenomenon to its viewers.

For example, a January 2012 report on the KLXY-4 TV news in Spokane, Washington, opened like this:

Anchorwoman: "A Spokane man is offering to place a permanent advertisement on his body for just $5,000."

Anchorman: "Yeah, listen to this. Pete Taylor is the owner of SAVORx, that sells whole spices. He says he's tried every venue to jumpstart his company but he's been unsuccessful. Taylor says he'll get a person or a company's name tattooed on his back . . ."

Pete Taylor, a chef in Spokane, had cooked up a cockamamie stunt to bring attention to SAVORx, his Kickstarter project to deliver fresh spices and spicy recipes to backers. For a $5,000 pledge, he offered to tattoo any person's or business's name on his body. (He put the same offer on eBay.) He didn't get the pledge—but he got the publicity.

"Unless you know someone in the media, it is hard to find someone do a story on your Kickstarter project," he says. "So I added a couple elements to my campaign that would hopefully stick out like a sore thumb. The 'Ghost Pepper' [another stunt in which he had a video shot of him eating a painfully hot pepper] and my 'human billboard' got me in the local newspapers four or five times, on the local news, and on a few blogs. It was a ton of investigating, cold calls, cold e-mails, follow-ups. But we did get attention. It was worth it, too. I had so many people get in touch with me from it. One guy called the restaurant I work at as a chef, asking for 'Pete the spice guy.' He wanted to send me a check for a hundred bucks and wanted me to keep it no matter if my Kickstarter succeeded or failed. He sent the check that week. So the moral is: add an extra element to your project so the media might pick it up."

Public events work, too

It may be easy to overlook one obvious idea. Even though your Kickstarter campaign is online, you can still create a fund-raising event that happens in real life, assembling actual human beings in a real place. You know, like a party. Many successful Kickstarter project creators have staged fund-raising events during their campaigns. You need a local constituency who will attend, and you don't want to add too much cost to the project, but it can work.

There are two approaches to running a Kickstarter fund-raising event. Either offer the event as a reward, meaning that everyone who pledges a certain amount receives a ticket to attend. Or organize a free event where the plan is to excite attendees about your project and get them to pledge afterward (or during). For **Jekyll and Hyde:**

The Music Video, the music group Theoretics set up a free party in Seattle. The band played all night and hung out with attendees; they also, conveniently, had a computer opened to their Kickstarter donation page. For a Kickstarter documentary film project called **A Sustainable Reality: Redefining Roots**, creators required a $20 fee to attend a party in Chicago that featured many performers.

Some people who are moved to give you financial support at a fund-raiser may want to hand over the money directly rather than pledge via Kickstarter. That's perfectly legal (it's not like side deals between eBay buyers and sellers, which are prohibited). This offline interaction avoids the fees subtracted by Kickstarter and Amazon, but it won't count toward your Kickstarter goal. To support his **SAVORx** food project, Pete Taylor boosted both his Kickstarter pledges and his outside donations by holding an event called Spiceology 101 at a wine-tasting room in Spokane, near the end of his campaign. "I put a reward on Kickstarter: pledge $15 and receive a ticket. We sold about thirty-five tickets," he says. "At the event, I think five or six people wrote me a check for $100 because they liked what I was doing."

And don't forget that you can become involved in events that someone else is throwing: block parties, beer fests, conventions of enthusiasts, Occupy rallies. Target the most appropriate ones—those whose attendees will most likely relate to or be interested in your project. Then contact the organizers and see how best to partner for mutual success—they may appreciate the buzz your participation will bring, and you will benefit from reaching their built-in audience.

The chosen ones: Is there a way to be featured by Kickstarter?

Being featured by Kickstarter's own gatekeepers—as a "Staff Pick" or "Project of the Day" —can be a huge boon to a campaign. Then again, it may not make one iota of a difference.

"I think we got funded about two-thirds of the way through,

mostly because Kickstarter featured us on their main page," says Josh Hartung, cocreator of the **Loomi** lamp-kit project. "Once that hit, it was like a fire hose. For the last third of the project, we were making approximately $2,500 a day."

By contrast, Abbey Londer, whose campaign raised money to start the **RIOT** comedy festival in Los Angeles, says that being featured as Kickstarter Project of the Day created "hardly any bump" in her fund-raising. Why? She figures that her project had so much purely local appeal, that having the world know about it might not have been a big deal.

Either way, there's no point in worrying about a factor you can't control. There's really nothing you can do to get Kickstarter's staff to choose to highlight your campaign, short of having a cool, popular, and successful project that's worthy of attention and already bringing in pledges. Even then, you need to get lucky.

What Do Bloggers Look for When Covering Kickstarter Projects?

Tina Roth Eisenberg, Swissmiss.com

New York–based designer Tina Roth Eisenberg started the Swissmiss blog (swiss-miss.com) in 2005 as a way to save visual ideas from around the Web. "I wanted to sort of archive my findings in a visual way, because I couldn't find stuff in my bookmarks folder," she says. "It started as a personal visual archive, and it has grown into something massive that I could have never imagined." The site now has about 900,000 unique visitors a month. Eisenberg frequently highlights Kickstarter projects that intrigue her, often simply posting their video with a little comment. Campaigns such as **Pen Type-A** and **Freaker** blew up after a nod from Swissmiss. Here are a few words from Tina about her approach to featuring Kickstarter projects on Swissmiss.

What catches your attention in a Kickstarter campaign?

Eisenberg: Well, there's an art to making a good Kickstarter video. The first few seconds are crucial for me to stay and watch it or not. There are definitely people who have it down. Sometimes I see an idea that's good, but the execution of the video is horrendous. But really it comes down to a gut reaction: Is the idea strong? Is the intention of the people good? Sometimes I get a sense when makers are really passionate. Then I get really carried away in my enthusiasm for the campaign.

Do you do a "Kickstarter of the week" or regular feature like that?

Eisenberg: No. It has to do with me browsing the Kickstarter site or getting pitched via e-mail.

You browse a lot?

Eisenberg: Our running joke, here in the coworking space I started, is that going on the Kickstarter site for me is way more dangerous than walking into Soho. Most of us are not really interested in acquiring more stuff—we're interested in ideas and makers. So I'm much more prone to leave way too much money on Kickstarter, backing way too many projects. It's been around thirty. Then I get my credit card statement at the end of the month! Walking into a mall I wouldn't care so much about shopping. I just want to support good ideas.

You must get a lot of people approaching you about featuring the Kickstarter campaigns . . .

Eisenberg: At this point the rate of Kickstarter projects I'm getting pitched by e-mail has gone up to between five and ten a day. Even as someone who helps promote them, I'm starting to get tired of being pitched. And I'm a big fan of the site. Usually when people who have Kickstarters e-mail me, it has this other layer of personal note. It says, *Here's why I really, really care for this to succeed, and can you help me?* If I sense the enthusiasm, the passionate spark for what they're doing, then I'm also more intrigued to look at it.

Are you cognizant of the impact Swissmiss has on some Kickstarter campaigns?

Eisenberg: Having the massive readership I have now, which is so mind-boggling, I feel I need to put it to good use and help people who are starting out. When you have readers like I do, it's amazing what kind of impact you can have on someone's life. I have posted a lot of other things—not just Kickstarter—people who have an idea for a product, maybe they start making a product selling on Etsy, and I pick it up, and I get an e-mail a day later, like, *Oh my god, I was sold out in an hour; now I'm considering making this my full-time career.* To be honest, I kind of get a high on all that. And it's a little scary.

The Tech Perspective

Seattle-based writer Devin Coldewey has been a contributor to TechCrunch since 2007 and been featured by one blog as a "geek we love." He has written about multiple Kickstarter projects.

How do you find out about the Kickstarter stuff you write about?

Coldewey: It's kind of a mix. We tend to scroll through the newest Kickstarter entries. We get pitched sometimes, into our e-mail inbox. We have a "tip line." Sometimes stuff is directed just to me, if it's something I've covered. I think I've written up a few camera accessories on Kickstarter, so those kinds of things. Sometimes we know of the people involved, heard of them before, and they're like, *Hey, I'm about to launch a Kickstarter campaign!*

Sometimes you hear about stuff after it's already starting to blow up, and the story is more that it has momentum, rather than the story being, *here's this thing, let's give it some momentum.* But we're always scraping the Web for interesting stuff, on Kickstarter and other sites. There isn't a dedicated story-finder on the staff for these bubbleup stories. We look around and are aware of what's interesting to our readers, what will bring traffic, of course, what's a good or bad Kickstarter.

What is a good or bad Kickstarter—from the perspective of a tech blog?

Coldewey: Well, another iPad case? Not so much. But something that's really interesting is worth posting, no matter what. Just being on Kickstarter isn't enough. It used to be, *Ooh, so you're trying that whole Kickstarter thing?* Nowadays if you're an entrepreneur, if you've got an idea, it's almost weird if you're not considering putting it on Kickstarter. There are plenty of things that you'll see and think, *wow, that is a really great idea.* A lot of things like gadgets or software that has a sort of niche audience, you can see why they're not being manufactured en masse, but there is a global audience. If someone's trying to offer it and they've got a good design, a good team, a good pedigree, that's a good example of what Kickstarter is for.

Is there a good way for someone to pitch a Kickstarter campaign to you?

Coldewey: It depends a lot on the quality of the product. The best way to pitch it is to make it seem most like a Kickstarter project.

In what way?

Coldewey: Not just, *we're using Kickstarter,* but, *this is a project that's suitable for Kickstarter.* Where it's like, *we've got a cool idea and we want to make it, but we have no ability to make it, and all it takes is $20,000.* That's the purpose of Kickstarter. If you can't convince me that Kickstarter is the right way to connect with people for your product, then it seems wrong. If you're trying to make a hundred hand-quilted iPad cases or whatever, why don't you put it on Etsy and make them on demand? There's a marketplace for doing that.

And Now a Word from a Professional Publicist

Jennifer Sherlock, founder and president of Jenna Communications, a public relations and media training firm in Philadelphia, has spread the news for start-up companies, planned and publicized events, and trained clients in the use of social media. She also worked as a full-time on-camera TV news reporter for seven years. She shared her advice about getting publicity for individual projects.

If I'm just a guy with a Kickstarter project and I don't know anybody in the media, where do I start?

Sherlock: Look at press-release templates and create a release. You need to explain the project and make it newsworthy. You may not have access to reporters by personal acquaintance, but you can easily use Google to find them. You can Google five TV stations in each market and hit the relevant newspapers. [Google can help with press-release templates, too: "Kickstarter press release" turns up quite a few examples.] E-mail the press release to them. Don't be afraid to be persistent. When you find the right reporter to write to, be personal. A reporter likes you to say, *I watch you or I know someone who knows you.* Don't be afraid. It's just like sales. Once you send the initial pitch or press release, don't be afraid to call.

So, if I know the person I'm trying to reach, should I e-mail, then call?

Sherlock: E-mail first nowadays. So they're familiar with the story. Then call.

How about a TV station? Do I just cold-call them?

Sherlock: For TV, I would recommend cold-calling the station first and asking for the news desk. The news desk is the hub for all incoming news. An assignment editor can direct the caller to the right producer or reporter for the story. It's important that the caller targets the person who is most relevant to their story. A consumer reporter may be helpful if the person has a product and is trying to get publicity.

How are people using social media to get PR buzz?

Sherlock: Any time you get a press hit, you should put it on your website, on Facebook, Twitter, LinkedIn. That gives credibility and is another opportunity to remind people that the campaign is going on. Even create a YouTube channel. Add videos there, and then post them on Facebook.

How important is it for someone to make their project into a story?

Sherlock: It's 100 percent the biggest thing to do. The best thing to do is to make it personal. I know just from being a TV reporter in my past, we always tell the story through the people. If they can personalize it, show a success story. If it's TV, you want to make the story visual—why is it a good TV story? If it's print, you can still paint the story visually to make it compelling. For example, I had a hypnosis center as a client. You know, it's hard—he does hypnotism! We had to think outside the box. Last year we contacted Fox TV and said, *We can show how he helped someone with their golf swing.* So we could take them to a golf course, they could see how he hypnotizes a client. They had something to show on camera.

9.

THE FINISHING KICK

It's time to cross the goal line—plus four frantic finishes

"The best statistic—I hope you put this in 72-point type across two pages—is that once you pass 50 percent of your funding, at any point, you have a 95 percent chance of reaching your goal. There's a human psychology element where people go, yeah I'll kick in more, this guy's so close. Only a handful of projects have finished unsuccessfully having reached 85 percent or more of their funding. The people who are at like 60, 70 percent with a week to go, it's gonna be OK!"

—Matt Haughey

YES, IT CAN LOOK BLEAK in the final days of a Kickstarter campaign if you haven't yet passed your goal, if even spitting distance seems like many miles down the road. But if you've set a goal that's anywhere near realistic, you still have a shot. Here's the pep talk you need. You're not out of this thing, kid. Just a few more days of effort and you can achieve something incredible—everything you've been working for. Need more inspiration? Here are four real-life Kickstarter stories of incredible final-days comebacks. They'll surely provide motivation, and great ideas, for your final kick.

Frantic Finish #1

In early December 2010, filmmaker Lucas McNelly launched a 31-day Kickstarter campaign to raise $12,000, for a project called **A Year Without Rent**. His exact creative plans for the project were a little vague. The basic idea was that he was going to travel across the country for a year, working on diverse independent films, and he'd document his travels. Weeks went by after he launched, and it wasn't looking good. The response, pledge-wise, was close to crickets. He said in his appealing video that he was more interested in the crowd than the funding, but he was drawing neither. As the new year arrived and the deadline crept close enough for Lucas to feel its cold, clammy breath, he was still nowhere near his goal. He steeled himself for a final climb up a steep mountain. It took a Hail Mary post-Christmas miracle (and lots of eleventh-hour work) to pull off what may be the biggest late-inning rally in Kickstarter history.

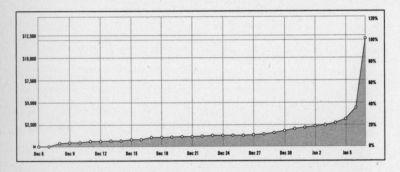

How far away were you from your goal, how close to the deadline?

McNelly: We were 73 percent away with twenty-four hours to go. Which is a little nuts.

Some might see that as a good time to throw in the towel . . .

McNelly: Yeah. Well, I mean, sure. But you've already invested, like, two and a half months of your life in it, so why give up now? My family would call and say, *What are you gonna do if it doesn't make it?* I'm like, *Can you maybe ask me this tomorrow? Can we put that conversation off for, like, a day, until we know for sure?* I think the minute you say *this probably isn't gonna happen* is the minute it isn't gonna happen.

So what did happen? What did you do? What can people learn from your experience?

McNelly: Well, the biggest thing is, I screwed up and I ran the campaign over Christmas. I thought Christmas will knock out three or four days when nothing will happen. But it's really about two weeks. So that stunted the normal growth. The campaign ran through the second Friday after Christmas. I remember because, when I scheduled it, I said to myself: that will give everybody at least one paycheck after Christmas.

Also the project was a weird concept. I think it took a while for people to figure out what the hell I was raising money for. There were people who backed it who would ask me two weeks later, *so, what the hell did I just back?*

It really felt like being the show runner for *Arrested Development*. It seemed like everyone influential in the independent film world was saying, *back this campaign, it's going to be cool.* And no one was backing it. I think what happened was that somebody finally took their finger out of the dam, and it was just, boom. It exploded.

But you must've really intensified the amount of tweeting and other things you were doing toward the end.

McNelly: Yeah. I got kicked off Twitter, which I didn't know you could do. We were going pretty hard. For the final three days, we did sleep strikes every day and had blog posts running everywhere.

What's a sleep strike?

McNelly: A sleep strike is when, say you're at ninety backers at eleven o'clock at night, and you get yourself and two other people to stay up until you hit one hundred backers. You just refuse to go to sleep. You just keep tweeting it and tweeting it and tweeting it. It's kind of stupid, because nobody's awake. But people hear about it later. When they get up. It shows a level of dedication. So we were up until like five a.m. each of those nights.

At that late point, were you going back to your friends or trying to find new outlets?

McNelly: My goal was to find new people. I kind of knew before I did the project that I was gonna need an audience anyway. It wasn't going to do any good to have somebody write a big check. I was telling people I would rather have 12,000 $1 backers than one $20,000 backer, because I needed that audience. My thing was pushing out further and further and finding new people.

How down to the wire did you get?

McNelly: I think we hit the goal with one minute left, two minutes left. I had a friend who had said, *Look, if you get to within two grand, I can bail you out.* But we were so far behind, she gave up and went to a bar. I texted her with a half hour left, and she was like, *Oh my gosh, I can't get home in time. You were six grand behind when I left.* I said, *yeah, it's kind of been busy.* It got kind of furious at the end. I think we got about forty-nine backers in the last hour. My tweetdeck was spinning like the wheel on *The Price Is Right.*

Frantic Finish #2

In May 2011, with seven days to go in her campaign, Aurora Guerrero was $50,258 short of her goal of raising $80,000 for *Mosquita Y Mari*, a feature film about two Latina teenagers who develop a romantic relationship. With two days remaining, she was still about $40,000 away. She almost gave up but didn't. Here's what she did instead.

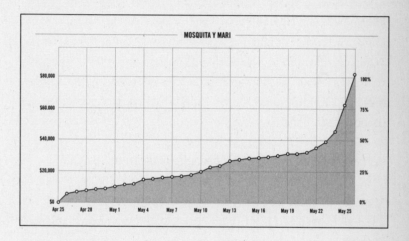

What were you thinking, being so far behind with so little time left?

Guerrero: In those forty-eight hours, I was an emotional wreck. I was really trying to keep the faith, you know? But at the same time, I'm a strategist, and I'm also a filmmaker. And I gotta be in the real. I was like, forty-eight hours out, forty grand down, man! Odds are against us. What are we gonna do? Myself and my producers were already developing a follow-up Kickstarter campaign with a lower goal. What we were hoping was that, if in the end we got $45,000, we'd launch a new campaign right on the heels of it and say, *we know we can raise $45,000, and that's what our goal is, and we need to recommit.* It was scary—to have to ask people to redonate. I knew that we were going to lose people. The momentum is going to feel different. We had the backup campaign already built and everything. We just had to publish it, and my finger was on that button. I was going to announce it in the last forty-eight hours. I was gonna tell people, *Look, let's not lose hope. We have a backup campaign.* I was gonna make that announcement.

But there was a woman who was a part of my team—she was making more personal connections and had a network that was a little more lucrative than mine, bigger donors. In the last forty-eight hours some of her donors hadn't come through. I told her, *We're just gonna announce that we have a backup campaign,* and she was like, *No, don't do it, they're gonna think you're losing faith. You've gotta hold on, we're gonna make it.* And I listened, and I didn't do it. And her donors came through.

You really believed you had a chance to make the $80,000?

Guerrero: I knew that word of mouth was spreading. We had already raised $40,000. And I felt that to raise $40,000 was already amazing. That is a big chunk of money that was on the table. I thought, *are we just going to let that pass?* I was definitely looking at it as a gambler. I come from a family of gamblers, and I was thinking, *no way the community can't walk away from $40,000.* I was presenting it as such: *If we don't make $80,000, we lose $40,000.* It was too big to lose.

What were your tactics?

Guerrero: If you have a large network of people you have relationships with, either directly or one degree or two degrees of separation, you know people. That community is ultimately your audience. I knew that I had a big community. I've been building this network since I was nineteen and started working in different communities around social justice issues. So, I went out to the communities that I had built, and I sent them e-mails, and I Facebooked them and was like, *Hey, this is happening. We've raised forty grand and we have a deadline, and I need your support. I need you to not only give but to spread the word to your network of people.* I took the time to write a little blurb that talked about me and the film and what we were doing. I put that as part of the e-mail, so they could grab it and put it in an e-mail that they would generate or post on Facebook. I tried to make it as easy as possible for my networks to spread the word.

We had a team built around this campaign. Myself, one of my producers, and another young woman who is very savvy about social media, who worked for an organization called Presente.org. They organize people around social issues that affect Latinos, using online campaigns. She is one of the people behind that, and she is brilliant. I approached her, and said, *I need your brilliance.* After she read the script for the film, she decided to be part of the team. She helped construct an online campaign for it. She also had relationships with bloggers and press people. So she said, *Let's develop a press kit so they can write about it.* We put it out there like, *Look, this is newsworthy. This filmmaker is turning to her community for help.* We created that sort of media-worthy event, and people picked it up. We had it blogged. *La Opinion*, a Spanish-language newspaper, picked it up and did a story. We strategized with them about when they would release it.

What happened late in the campaign to turn it around?

Guerrero: I'm Latina, and in communities of color we say that we run on "people of color time." In other words, sometimes, you know, we're last-minute-type people! I feel like that happened. A lot of people at the beginning of the campaign hadn't given—they had e-mailed me to let me know that they were gonna give, but they didn't tell me when. Time passed, and next thing it was forty-eight hours left! A lot of reminders went out: *All right folks, here it is, now is the time.* And then they really went out to their networks and started pitching the project. We had two donors who each donated $5,000. One had donated throughout—she spread it out throughout the campaign. The other was one whole chunk at the very end.

It was hard work, but there is some magic in it that I will never be able to put words to. I felt like it was the universe saying: *it's time.* After Kickstarter, we were at full speed. You have to pay attention to momentum. We wrapped the film—we went into preproduction for June and shot in July for eighteen days. Our Kickstarter was to help us get through production; it didn't include postproduction. We had applied to the San Francisco Film Society for postproduction funds. We were literally writing grants as we were shooting. We got that postproduction grant and went into post in August and were in post through October before we submitted to Sundance. *[Mosquita Y Mari was selected to screen at the Sundance Film Festival, and Guerrero sold distribution rights to the film there.]*

Frantic Finish #3

On Valentine's Day 2012, five days before his campaign to raise $12,000 would end, Pete Taylor was getting a little desperate. A restaurant chef from Coeur D'Alene, Idaho, working in Spokane, Washington, Taylor had launched his **SAVORx** food project on Kickstarter hoping to offer fresh spices and recipes to backers. The campaign gained traction like a truck in mud. About halfway in, when he was about 25 percent funded, his "white knight" big-money donor put in $5,000, injecting that bump into the middle of the campaign rather than waiting until the end. They hoped it would change the trajectory of the funding curve—and maybe the surge would get Kickstarter to put the campaign on one of its highlight pages. But the big donation was its own blip, and the painfully slow growth resumed.

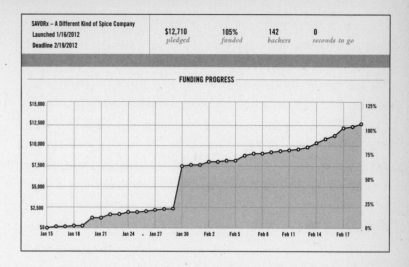

SAVORx – A Different Kind of Spice Company
Launched 1/16/2012
Deadline 2/19/2012

$12,710 *pledged* | 105% *funded* | 142 *backers* | 0 *seconds to go*

FUNDING PROGRESS

By February 14, with five days to go, the campaign was up to 83 percent funded—about $9,900—and grinding ahead in tiny steps. "It's crazy stressful," Taylor wrote in an e-mail message. "We are so close, but I have totally exhausted my resources. Between Facebook/ Twitter/local media/YouTube/etc.... there is not much more I can do. It already seems spam(ish). I have e-mailed Kickstarter and asked them for help in homepage placement or blog placement, but it is always the same generic reply: 'Everyone wants to be on the homepage, sorry.'" He even watched as $150 worth of pledges was withdrawn.

Maybe because he's a spice guy, grinding turned out to be Taylor's strength. He persevered and did what it took to reach his goal.

Who ended up coming through for you? Did you go to friends and family or kind strangers?

Taylor: Ironically, it seems like friends and family helped out the least. Maybe it's just me. Acquaintances helped out a decent amount, and then total strangers were great. I guess it's not a fair comparison, because you have the whole Kickstarter community, and they're already exposed to what projects are about and are more apt to pledge. I was on Facebook finding foodie groups, attaching links to my Kickstarter project. With all the networking, and all the promotion through Facebook, Twitter, cold calling, e-mailing however many thousands of e-mails I sent, the result was that family and friends are less likely to pledge than people you know just a tiny bit. Maybe you met them, you're sort of friends on Facebook. Small-business owners, corporate-type individuals, marketers, social media people. They're the people who really supported the campaign. I didn't have one family member go to our fund-raising event, but I had probably about thirty people I'd never met in my life show up.

Did anything else help with momentum?

Taylor: Toward the end, we got a bit of Kickstarter action. I think we started to get higher up in the "popular" list in the food category, so pledges were coming from within Kickstarter. There were $100 pledges from people I'm not affiliated with. People I had never met who found out about my project; the more I talked to them they just went crazy over it. One guy originally pledged $25, then he changed it to $75, then $100, and then $150. He also wrote these great comments.

So, things were iffy for a while, but you really pushed through it . . .

Taylor: The moment I pressed Launch, for the next thirty-three days it was pure . . . intensity. Having to work a real job and trying to promote this campaign at the same time. I found out the hard way that it's a lot of work if you want it to be successful.

Frantic Finish #4

Even when he was tens of thousands of dollars shy of his goal, and with his deadline looming, Bill Lichtenstein stayed upbeat about his campaign to raise funds to make **The American Revolution**, a documentary about seminal Boston rock radio station WBCN. His target of $104,000 was ambitious. About halfway through the campaign, with fourteen days left, he was at only 28 percent of the goal. On December 5, 2011, with five days to deadline, he was more than $40,000 short. But his team kept pushing, and he had one last trick up his sleeve: recruiting the endorsement of a beloved local athlete.

You were confident all the way through, but how did you pull it off?

Lichtenstein: I can give you ten different theories about why it went the way it did. It's sort of like Election Day, in that the only thing that matters is reaching people, getting them to donate. So we just kept reaching out to people, seeking publicity. We kept trying to expand the circle. On Facebook. We got a lot of press. We got the trifecta of Boston media, which is a piece in the *Globe*, a long piece in the *Boston Herald*, and then *Chronicle*, the TV show on Channel 5 that covers everything cultural in the city. It became a seven-day news cycle. That started about halfway through the campaign.

What got you to the end? Small donations, one big whale?

Lichtenstein: One thing we learned is that there was no one homerun ball. There was no one thing. Though in the end, I should say, what closed it out was Bill Lee [the fan-favorite former Red Sox pitcher nicknamed "Spaceman"]. He sent out an e-mail for us telling people to pledge to the project. Obviously, we reached out to him. He had just helped with another Kickstarter—for a film about him. We thought we'd have to explain it to him, but he said, *Oh, I just did a Kickstarter;*

they're great. That e-mail was on December 16, and our campaign was scheduled to end on the nineteenth. We knew we had to find some way to close it out, because we were heading into a holiday weekend and a potential blizzard; a million things that could happen. His e-mail went out to everybody on my e-mail list for the last ten years. It was like, *go for it.* About ten thousand people. People on the e-mail list from our old public radio show. Our old FedEx representative in New York, whom I hadn't talked to in four years, gave ten dollars. It had the right tone to it. You can't be frantic. It was just the idea of him coming in and saying, *let's close this thing out.* [Lee's message said: "When I played for the Red Sox, I was a 'BCN listener, and we knew that together we were helping to change our world."] That created the final $5,000 to $10,000 burst over those two days.

It's a commitment to hit up everyone you ever knew! You really have to want it.

Lichtenstein: I would say it's like running for office. You can't, on Election Day, be going, *well, I'm not sure if I really want to be the senator.* You have to be out there 100 percent, saying, *look, we gotta do this thing, this has to happen, we need your help,* please *do what you can.* Anything other than that, you're not gonna make it. There are kids now who create a gadget that everybody wants—a bike lock that you can't steal or something—and they presell them on Kickstarter for $20 apiece, and if people want to buy them, you can raise a lot of money very fast. But for films, or for things that are more mission oriented, you have to approach it in the same way as you would if you were asking people for money the old-fashioned way. Be sincere, be serious, be humble.

We a made a decision—it was right before Christmas, and there was such a good vibe. After we passed our goal, we sort of stopped asking people to give. We were happy with what we had. I thought to keep it going at that point would be too much.

10.

AFTER THE LOVING:
TALES OF FULFILLMENT

Delivering the goods to your generous backers

S O YOUR PROJECT has been successfully funded. It becomes official when the deadline for your campaign has passed. You did it! A Kickstarter update to your backers— with a giant thank-you—is appropriate to post at this moment. And, soon thereafter, an update on what your donors can expect next.

The battle has been won. Dozens, hundreds, maybe even thousands of fans have let you know, with their wallets and their words, how much they want you to push ahead with your dream. They have validated your creative instincts and your talent. A new phase of rewarding work has begun.

Just when you thought the hard work was over comes still more hard work. Issuing rewards to backers is both a blessing and a curse. That you need to do it means that you have succeeded in your Kickstarter campaign. The process of sending out rewards is happily called "fulfillment." But it can also be a serious expense and a logistical challenge. Your goal is to prevent it from escalating into "nightmare" territory. Success has snuck up on some Kickstarter campaign creators, and the results aren't always pretty. One day you're an artist or designer looking to fund your dream, and the next day you're trying to figure out how to manufacture 4,000 alarm clocks.

That's a wake-up call.

What happens after you succeed is simple enough. Kickstarter sends you a message that your campaign has ended successfully. Since you already set up an Amazon Payments account when you launched your campaign (see chapter 7, "The Kickoff!"), you will soon be able to access the money. Amazon charges your backers' credit cards for the amounts they have pledged, taking 3 to 5 percent of the total for credit-card processing fees. Amazon also sends Kickstarter 5 percent of the amount you raised. You get the rest. So if you've raised $10,000 in pledges, you might collect slightly more than $9,000. Note that it takes a little while to get the money. Amazon may hold funds for up to fourteen days after payments are collected, and it could take up to another five business days for the funds to transfer to your bank account.

As a successful campaign creator, you will be able to send a postcampaign survey to all your backers requesting their shipping addresses and product preferences, that is, if they have choices to make (colors, sizes, and the like). Kickstarter provides you with a spreadsheet containing all of your backers' information, and you can use that list to produce mailing labels, or hand-address packages, or give the spreadsheet to a fulfillment center that will handle shipping logistics for a fee. You have only one opportunity to send out this official survey, so some campaign creators, instead of sending it out immediately, will wait until their rewards are ready to ship, ensuring that they will have gathered the most current addresses for all recipients and know exactly what the product options will be. You can continue to reach all your backers by e-mail through the Kickstarter website and by posting updates on the project page. Some creators have opted not to use Kickstarter's survey and instead collected backer information by creating customized surveys using Google Forms that can be e-mailed. Google Forms are free and also dump all responses into a handy spreadsheet.

What happens next is different for each person. The real-life experiences of Kickstarter creators who have encountered the spoils of success speak loudly. You can learn plenty from their reward-fulfillment strategies as well as their miscalculations. Here are their stories.

"The shipping was quite an undertaking."

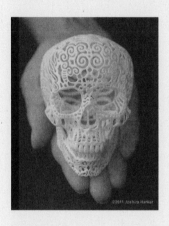

Chicago artist Joshua Harker received an unbelievable, and unexpected, response to his **Crania Anatomica Filigre** project in October 2011. Harker creates ornate sculptures that he calls "tangles." Many of his designs had been "unmakeable" using traditional sculpture methods in the days before the existence of computers and 3-D printing. As rewards in his campaign, he offered an awesome-looking skull sculpture: $50 for a small one, $100 for a medium size, and $250 for a large. He set a low bar, seeking to raise just $500 total, but then proceeded to rake in $77,271 from 955 backers, becoming at the time the third most highly funded art project in Kickstarter history. After that overwhelming success came the task of getting all those skulls to all those generous backers.

"The shipping was quite an undertaking," Harker says. "You don't realize during the project that you may get more than you bargained for. You may expect a certain number, but when it's thousands of times more than that—mine was 15,454 percent funded—where do you begin to organize? I wonder if Kickstarter should offer an option for the creators to end a project after a certain amount of money/backers has been received without canceling it. [Author note: there is a way to limit availability of any reward, which can effectively achieve the same goal of limiting the artist's postcampaign obligations.] For some, too much of a good thing can sabotage their ability to accomplish the project as designed. For the most part, we're talking about small-time artists trying to break out. Not many are set up for the logistics of managing a large-scale project that some of these campaigns turn into—manufacturing, shipping and receiving, inventory, quality control, customer service.

"The type of rewards I offered were not difficult for me to fulfill. I had worked with the mediums and the vendors many times, and all the design work was already complete. I have an account [with the fabricator] where I upload my designs to get pricing, in whatever materials they offer. I simply order whatever quantities of my designs I need, and in about three weeks they show up at my door. Honestly, all I had to do was collect the money, order the corresponding rewards, and ship them out.

"I didn't get a volume discount, since the company bases its pricing on volume processing. I did get priority attention, as far as project management and delivery. I had a couple vendors lined up, one in the Netherlands and one in New Zealand, but ended up using just one because of some practical matters. So they were printed and then sent to me on pallets. I repacked everything and shipped via the U.S. Postal Service.

"The addresses were provided by Kickstarter via a spreadsheet at the end of the project. I used a computer to print labels, but I had to fill out about 300 customs labels by hand. I also included a personalized hand-written postcard in all the packages. I packed everything manually. I pushed to get everything shipped and delivered before Christmas, including all the orders that came in shortly after the project ended. The post office was a bit of a circus, given that it happened to be the holiday rush. We took the packages in batches, as they were packed. Out of a thousand packages, only three have 'disappeared' into post office ether, and one was crushed. I consider that a low percentage. It proved to be a tight squeeze, but we did it.

"I'm certainly making it sound easier than it was. But, considering the corners some creators on Kickstarter get themselves into, I think it went exceptionally smooth."

"A lot of people get overextended."

Jacob Krupnick asked for $4,800 to make **Girl Walk // All Day**, a high-energy feature-length film showing dancers in public locations throughout New York City.

He raised $24,871 in a 45-day Kickstarter campaign. That would have been one of the biggest dance projects in Kickstarter history (and it sort of is, but Krupnick assigned the project to the Film category). He offered DVDs of the movie to backers at the $30 pledge level and tickets to a New York premiere to $100 donors. He ended

up spending more than he raised and encountered one reward that was especially difficult to fulfill because it was so popular. Months after the campaign ended, he gave us a status update:

"I feel like a lot of people get overextended with what they promise backers as far as rewards. That's dangerous territory.

For us, it was DVDs and tickets for attending the premiere. In a perfect world, your project produces the rewards. But really the film doesn't produce DVDs. We have to produce them.

"The biggest issue was that we promised people tickets to the premiere. People could get one or two or four. In my humble mathematics, a great turnout might mean that we'd have 100 or 200 people to show the film to. At that scale, you can find a bar or a rooftop in New York that is pretty doable, or cheap, or sort of free, if you play your cards right. Then you take that money you've allotted, and you put it toward a keg, and you rent a sound system, and you have a good old time.

"Since we had really wonderful reaction to the project, there were 577 people who donated. About 500 tickets to the premiere were promised through Kickstarter. But by the time we'd made the film, it was more like 800 people, because so many people had had a hand in it. The unofficial friends list was another 220 or 300. At that scale, nothing in New York is free. We struggled with that. We were running up against the date when we were hoping to premiere the film. For a while we had what looked like a surefire partnership with a great space, a photo studio. But after a bunch of exchanges, the line went cold and we didn't hear back from them. Spaces were several thousand dollars for the night, and the projector that I have wouldn't cover it. And with that many people, suddenly you need security. You need a big bar. You need insurance. You need lots of speakers. So we were sort of flummoxed. We had really reached an impasse. We would have had to do small screenings, or send apologies.

"At some point, conversations began with Kickstarter [also based in New York]. They were interested in partnering with us to throw a big public premiere dance party. We had 1,200 or more people there. I don't know how we would have done it otherwise."

"It turned out to be more [costly] than we expected."

Swarm, a design firm in Salt Lake City, had to try twice (see chapter 11, "Learning from Failure") to find Kickstarter success for its **Nectar and Elixir** bicycle seat clamps that double as beer-bottle openers. They offered Nectar, a bolt-on version, for a $20 pledge, and Elixir, the quick-release version, for $30. The chance to try a second time taught the firm's three principals enough to reach their fund-raising target, but when the time came to send out rewards, they once again found themselves riding on bumpy terrain. They had offered too many variations of the product and were forced to produce some in small, money-losing quantities. All in all, they lost money on their Kickstarter campaign, says Wesley Garrett, one of Swarm's partners.

"Yeah, it turned out to be more [costly] than we expected. We have a lot of experience in manufacturing, both domestically and internationally, so we felt like we had a really good handle on that. But it just kind of escalated. We didn't lose much. And we had product left over after the production run. We were able to sell it all and recoup those losses. But even if we were selling those products at a profit, we had lost so much—I mean the shipping costs, we hadn't really thought through. We had a lot of international customers.

"Our product had too many variations. We had four colors and we had four sizes, within two different products, the quick-release clamp and the bolt-on. Which means that we had a total of thirty-two products we had to deliver. The cost to make the green color—we hadn't estimated that only a few people would want green—we lost about ten bucks per product on that! My advice is: definitely keep the SKUs as few as possible!"

"The math is insane!"

Scott Thrift offered **The Present**, his colorful one-year clock, for a $120 pledge and sought to raise $24,000 in all. By the end, he raised $97,567 and needed to find a way to make far more clocks than he'd anticipated. Here is Thrift's story, told about two months after his campaign.

"I went in thinking that I was going to sell hopefully 100 clocks. Luckily, it went in a completely different direction and got a lot of press and a lot of attention. And it put us in a place where we have to produce many more than that—we're looking at producing 2,000 units right now.

"I sold these clocks all over the world. I was really myopic going into it, thinking I was going to sell 100. Thinking that only people in New York would want it. There was no way for me to prepare for that outcome. There's a humbleness for me to think I was going to sell 100. I was thinking that, in a month, hopefully with friends and family, we'd be able to push past the $24,000 mark. That was what I really believed. And three days later we had already passed that. In seventy-two hours, we passed the $24,000 mark. I was thinking about this as a market test, to see if there are people really interested in this product. What I wanted to do was take the proof that I'd sold 100 clocks to a gift show, maybe.

"The design of the clock was pretty difficult. We had to find a whiz kid in Brooklyn, through ITP [New York University's technology arts program]. The idea was to crack open the movement in the back of a regular clock, remove the circuit board that tells it to click every second, and create our own circuit board. That took months. The math is insane! I still can't wrap my head around it. The plan was to manually swap out the movement for each clock. But once we sold more than 1,200 clocks, that was taken off the table. I had to step back and figure out how to do this in a way that was totally reliable and would last for years on one battery charge. So now we're having an annual clock movement made. Instead of hacking clocks, I'm actually making one from the ground up."

"So, yeah, we have a lawyer now."

Chei-Wei Wang and Taylor Levy, partners in the Brooklyn design firm CW&T, got more than they bargained for in their Kickstarter campaign for **Pen Type-A: A minimal pen** during the Summer of 2011.

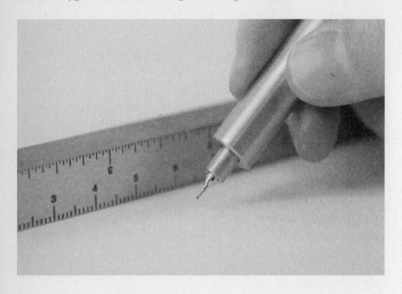

As product designers, they were aware of the successes that others had experienced with Kickstarter and were eager to try it. One concept they thought might work was an idea for a sleek stainless-steel pen that could hold cartridges made for the Pilot Hi-Tec-C pen, a writing implement they loved but that was sold in cheap, breakable plastic. They wanted something that would make their favorite pen more durable and comfortable to use. Thanks to a solid design and a great video (see chapter 6, "Lights, Camera, Action"), they won lots of attention and the campaign exploded. They set the pledge level for receiving one of the pens at $50 and put their total goal at just $2,500, which meant that they expected to make fifty pens. Instead of $2,500, they raised $281,989. And instead of 50 units, they attracted 4,449 backers and ended up needing to make and mail around 5,400 pens (some backers ordered more than one). Then came a long process of working to get the pens manufactured. Here's a conversation with both creators.

How soon did you realize this campaign was getting huge?

Taylor Levy: I guess the first day it got pretty big. The first day we reached our goal. We were totally overwhelmed and happy.

Chei-Wei Wang: We were so shocked. We didn't want to push it any further.

Levy: There were a lot of challenges. Manufacturing has been the biggest one. The most important thing we had to do was find a fabricator we could really communicate with, just to make sure we were all on the same page in terms of quality and they would hold themselves accountable.

We started off with the fabricator that made our prototypes, because we figured he can probably make 6,000 of these. But it turns out that making the small changes to improve them just a little bit, and making 6,000 of them consistently, is a whole different ballgame. They really weren't set up for that process. So we went over to China to figure that out. The manufacturer we're working with now is an American company with factories in China. To be perfectly honest, they're great, but they're also not set up to make something like this product. We've had to do a lot of work with them. But it's just like anything. We're all doing something new, we're all doing our best and learning from it.

What will you do with all the extra money you raised?

Levy: Right now, we don't know how much extra it is. Partly because we've made some mistakes. We paid one fabricator that didn't work out, and we're still trying to get our money back from that. There are also unexpected legal things that arise. So, yeah, we have a lawyer now and we have to pay him.

Wang: When we saw our friends Tom and Dan make a hundred-some-thousand dollars [designers Tom Provost and Dan Gerhardt raised $137,417 for an iPhone tripod called Glif], we were, like, *whoa, you can retire!* But now that we're in it, it's like, no, there's actually a lot of things you have to pay for.

Levy: We're going to get a bill from a fulfillment company for $70,000. What?! A $70,000 bill? Two years ago we were afraid of our $400 studio rent bill. This has kind of become our full-time thing now.

So you're still working on delivering the pens?

Levy: We just got our first shipment of 310 pens from our fabricators last week. We went though and did a bunch of quality-control tests. We found one little problem with all of them that we drilled and fixed on every single one. Also, they didn't properly clean the machine oil off the pens, so we had to wash them all, dry them, and assemble them. But we have about 280 pens now that are ready to ship.

Have backers waiting for pens grown impatient?

Levy: There's always going to be a couple of pretty vocal backers. *Who are you guys? What are you doing with all that money? Why is it taking you so long?* It's really way less than 1 percent of all the people. But it still really stresses me out. Luckily, our friends told us to wait as long as possible to send out the survey to get people's shipping addresses. You have one opportunity to send out a survey. Wait until the moment you're about to ship! Because if we had sent that survey out last August, we would have so many address changes.

Wang: We've been thinking about our next Kickstarter project, which is indefinitely on hold, and the idea of having a limited run, so it's not about trying to get as many preorders as you can. That would be nice.

"We wrote love notes on all our packages."

The folks behind the **Freaker** did an incredible job making a knit beer-bottle sock seem impossibly cool, and they took the bold step of offering one to anybody who gave even $1. They ended up needing to deliver about 2,400 packages.

"Twenty-four hundred packages is definitely a lot. It took a while, probably a couple months," says project leader Zach Crain. "And then you still have people messaging every once in a while: *Hey, I donated, I gave you guys money*. They had to fill out their surveys with their addresses. Some people thought that once they put in their credit cards, if it was successful it would just be shipped to them.

"Even on the $1 package, we sent it out in a yellow envelope, and we did a sort of cute little screenprint on it. We painted on all our boxes. We had white boxes and went over the surfaces with a roller. We wrote love notes on all our packages."

"Partner with the right people . . . even if sometimes it's not the path of least resistance."

David Sosnow and Josh Hartung prepared in advance for the success of their campaign for **Loomi** paper-lamp-making kits.

They raised $34,123 in December 2011. But even before they were done, the two were already getting ready. They had worked with a manufacturer to create customized tooling that would cut out the 33-piece paper-lamp kits.

"Our goal was to ship everything by Christmas," Hartung says. "David and I funded some production out of pocket, probably a

week and a half before we had achieved our funding goal. That's what I mean about planning for success. We had to take a risk there and plan that we were going to be successful. We had some ridiculous contingencies in case it didn't succeed, like, *I guess we can sell these at street fairs for the next year*."

When their project ended successfully on December 17, they needed to send out about 1,000 kits to about 600 backers. Because of the volume of rewards and the haste at which they needed to move, the pair worked with a fulfillment house to pack and ship everything.

"You provide them with the inventory and the address list, and they quote you a fee," Hartung explains. "They will charge you some flat fee to set up and maintain your account, and then they charge you per "touch." Usually it's like twenty-five cents per touch. A touch being if somebody pulls a unit of something that's yours and puts it into a box. They usually provide the boxes, and they have a charge for those, and packing materials, tape, all that. They also handle international shipping; they fill out all the customs forms."

Despite the excellent planning, it didn't go off without a hitch.

"We had sort of a fiasco," Hartung says. "We ended the campaign two days before the Christmas Priority Mail shipping cutoff. I ended up taking all the inventory to the fulfillment house from the manufacturer, and the fulfillment people sort of parsed it all out, but they messed up. They ended up double-shipping to a whole bunch of backers and not shipping to others.

"We shipped out our remaining inventory—there wasn't much—to the people who had gotten nothing, and our fulfillment company arranged a pickup with each person who had received a double delivery to return the extra inventory. We never even tracked how many we got back, because the company was so difficult to work with. In the end we paid them about a dollar each and moved all our fulfillment activities to another vendor. We were lucky because we had built in some margin that let us soak up that loss, but we still have upset backers who haven't gotten their rewards. Lesson: partner with the right people . . . even if sometimes it's not the path of least resistance."

11.

LEARNING FROM FAILURE

Kickstarter misfires, redemptions, and second acts

COMPUTER SCIENTIST ALAN KAY suggested that if you don't fail at least 90 percent of the time, you're not aiming high enough. That's pretty brutal math. Even amid those odds, Kay had his share of success. He conducted early work on graphical user interfaces, which every personal computer uses today, and he envisioned laptop and tablet computers before they existed. Given those accomplishments, you have to imagine he poured effort into lots of stuff that didn't work out so well.

Learning from failure is a reality of the creative process, a productive part of invention and entrepreneurship. All those things are the essence of Kickstarter. But learning from failure can be a jagged little pill, to borrow a phrase from another cultural commentator, Alanis Morissette. In this chapter we offer the next best thing to learning from your failure: learning from *other people's failure*.

Statistics released by Kickstarter note that, in 2011, 46 percent of campaigns succeeded. That's not Alan Kay territory, but it does mean that the majority of Kickstarter campaigns aren't winners. It means that, in 2011, more than 14,000 projects, in one way or another, crashed and burned. In fact, thanks to Kickstarter's rising popularity, more people are failing every year!

The reasons for the failures are diverse, but certain themes are repeated: Thinking that Kickstarter is a bizarro-world moneyland where you can get free cash for little effort. A lack of commitment to pressing acquaintances for backing. Reluctance to seek publicity. Having too little support lined up before launching a campaign. Poor presentation of the project, with a sloppy video or unfocused campaign page. Or, hey, just an idea that stinks or whose time has not yet come.

In the end, Kickstarter failure is all relative. The design firm Swarm failed in its first campaign for its **Nectar and Elixir** bicycle seat clamp/bottle openers. Their second try was a Kickstarter success but became a real-life failure, losing money and showing that the products themselves were not financially viable. In the big picture, however, the experience was a larger success, garnering valuable attention for the start-up design firm, quickly and at a low cost. Another case in point: a 2012 Kickstarter project called **graFighters** failed miserably, raising just $3,049 of its $20,000 goal. But the online game—which lets anyone upload a hand-drawn character and set it to battle against other people's doodles and illustrations—was pretty cool. So cool, in fact, that David Chenell and his cocreator Eric Cleckner, fresh off the Kickstarter defeat, were offered $200,000 from a venture capital firm. You never know what failure will bring.

As you think about launching your own Kickstarter effort, hearing what didn't work can be as helpful as gathering winning strategies. So, here are several campaigns that didn't succeed, with words of wisdom from the people behind those efforts. Also included are the voices of some creators who failed, retooled their idea, and then succeeded in their return engagements on Kickstarter.

These are their stories.

A Question of Ethics Podcast Series with Randy Cohen

Kickstarter goal: $25,000
Raised: $7,420

For twelve years, Randy Cohen was "The Ethicist" columnist in the *New York Times Magazine*, the Sunday publication of one of the most widely read newspapers in the United States. In his popular column, Cohen took questions from people dealing with ethical conundrums and helped them figure out how to behave. In 2011 he thought he'd expand his ethical expertise into a weekly, ten-minute podcast. To make it happen, he set out to raise $25,000 on Kickstarter. But despite his national prominence and media connections, Cohen's campaign raised less than $8,000, and he abandoned the podcast plan. He's now doing a non-ethics-focused public radio show called "Person Place Thing" and continues to provide moral support with his book *Be Good: How to Navigate the Ethics of Everything*.

So what happened with your Kickstarter campaign?

Cohen: We didn't hit our funding goal, but it's like being in a car accident, you know? There's an element of shame involved in it. I'm embarrassed. It was kind of public failure, and I feel slightly humiliated. But then you kind of feel your bones, like after an accident, to see if anything's broken. And I was pleased to find that I came out OK and really admire Kickstarter nonetheless. What they're doing is incredibly great. And I say this from the point of view of an abject failure.

What was your introduction to Kickstarter?

Cohen: I had met [Kickstarter cofounder] Perry Chen years ago, and he was talking about this idea where people would just give other people money for creative ideas. I remember thinking: *This kid is so bright and so nice, and so wrong about everything. This thing is doomed for failure. People aren't just going to give their money away.* Seldom does life let you be so unambiguously wrong. I was totally wrong, and he was utterly right.

Do you think your failure was about tactics or your overall idea?

Cohen: That's been hard to sort out. Sometimes the obvious explanation, however depressing and demoralizing to me personally, might be the correct one. And it's that maybe I wasn't nearly as popular as I thought. That could be the explanation. Given the chance to encourage me on the fine work I was doing, people said, "Eee, maybe not."

But that can't be true. Your column was hugely popular, in a magazine with a giant readership, right?

Cohen: Well, I do know this, and it sounds sort of braggy to mention it, but the *New York Times Magazine* has two million readers. I think it has a million subscribers, and there's some formula they use to calculate pass-along reads. And I know, because my powerful overlords told me repeatedly, that I was the most-read feature in the magazine. Of course, people might have read it with their fists clenched. But I know the column found readers. One explanation I considered is that maybe they're two separate audiences. Maybe the *Times* readership tends to skew a little bit older. I always imagine Kickstarter as skewing a little bit younger. So maybe they're two different groups.

Do you think your fund-raising target hampered your success?

Cohen: It did strike me that, for the kind of project we were doing, maybe we were aiming a little high. We raised $7,420. We were shooting for $25,000. And maybe that's too much for podcasts. Maybe the Kickstarter users are savvy about podcasts and think you should be able to do them for less money. Our task was to fund three months' worth of weekly podcasts, and the people I was working with were radio guys, radio producers who had a background in commercial radio. They were working on a budget in that context, with the idea of something highly produced. I though their ideas were good, but maybe that elaborate production, that works terrific as a show, for a podcast maybe it's a little excessive.

Do you think there was an issue with your rewards?

Cohen: I thought our rewards were pretty good. For the $250 pledge, the premium was "you be the announcer" in a podcast episode. We had three people choose that. And for the $500 level, it was "two drinks, two dilemmas." I'd meet with you and do a one-on-one private consultation. It seemed in-line with what other people were doing for similar projects. I know Kickstarter has done particularly well with design projects—where the reward you get is the thing itself. An early success was that beautifully designed watchband that turns your iPod nano into a wristwatch. We didn't have anything quite like that.

Do you think your video was too funny?

Cohen: I've been accused of the opposite! I tried to catch the tone of "The Ethicist" column but show how that might evolve a bit as a podcast. It was more explicitly funny than the column, but not by much. It wasn't that funny.

It was whimsical, and I wonder if people translated that as a lack of commitment? I wonder if potential backers can see the video and sense how much you really want it?

Cohen: Maybe you're crediting Kickstarter potential donors as having more psychological insight here than I would have figured. And I think maybe you're right. I was a little ambivalent about it going in. I had started working on a radio-show idea when I was still writing the column, and I had no idea that there was going to be a new editor taking over the magazine and firing me. But once that happened, by the time we got to the podcast and Kickstarter, I wasn't quite sure what to do next. Did I want to continue in the ethics biz? I had mixed feelings: it was a wonderful job, but maybe it was time to move on to other things. Maybe that came through.

Was there a point in the campaign where you weren't getting traction and sort of threw in the towel?

Cohen: No, no. At first I thought, *well, I have to get the word out more effectively.* At that point, I was no longer writing the column. So there's Facebook. I think some of my readers came over and liked my public figure page on Facebook. I tried to let people know. That was part of the process I never enjoyed, because it felt too much like begging your friends for money. Even to tell them about it. I wish there were a feature of Kickstarter that insulated you from that, that you were not permitted—this would be unenforceable— but it should be a guideline: you can't give money to anyone you know. You can define "know" as strictly as you wish. Do I have their home phone number? Have I had dinner at their house? Have I seen them naked? The same way you can't review a friend's book. And that would free me—because I wanted friends to tell other people about it. But I didn't at all like even telling my friends I was doing this, because it seemed like I was hitting them up for money. If Kickstarter incorporated that rule, the "no giving to close friends" rule, then I could tell everyone. Very few of my backers were close friends. It was more gratifying when strangers did it, because it sort of announced that they like your work.

Given your media connections, were you able to get good press?

Cohen: No, I don't think so. We might have had a little. Right, I suppose one mention by Oprah would do it! You know, you do this completely fallacious math, built on completely false premises: If only one out of every thousand Oprah watchers, or people who read the column, just gave two dollars! But that's just kidding-yourself math. We were never the featured project on Kickstarter, but they did write something about us on the blog. We couldn't have asked more from them. We really failed on our merits.

Do you think that, despite what you just said, if you had really, really wanted it, you could have made it work? If you were willing to ask friends for money, grovel for press, whatever it took?

Cohen: Yeah, maybe. Maybe that's true about almost any project. To really, really want the thing and be willing to do whatever it takes, whether or not some of those activities are unpalatable. Maybe I didn't do some things I might have done. I'm really enjoying my new radio show "Person Place Thing" on public radio. I would grovel for that. I would like to take it weekly and go national as soon as we can. Perhaps if I went on Kickstarter! *And this time. . . I'll get it right.*

Dreaming In Stainless
Kickstarter goal: $25,000
raised: $215

There have been, surprisingly, two different campaigns on Kickstarter to make documentary films about the legendary DeLorean automobile (you know, the futuristic stainless steel car with spread-eagle doors that was a star of sorts in the 1985 movie *Back to the Future*). One of the campaigns successfully hit its goal of $5,000, and the film (called *Back to the DeLorean* on Kickstarter and now *DeLorean: Living the Dream* on IMDB.com) went into production. Craig Werner's effort to raise $25,000 to make *Dreaming in Stainless*, a documentary about DeLorean owners, withered with just $215 pledged. We asked Werner what happened.

What do you think went wrong?

Werner: My feeling is that, taking a project to Kickstarter, you had better have a lot of support already, which this idea really didn't have. To gain momentum, you really have to have something in your pocket that you can take to it immediately. It picks up momentum, and then you're going to get more exposure through Kickstarter, because they like to promote successful projects.

How much work did you do to get attention for the campaign?

Werner: I sent a copy of the promo video to Jay Leno [knowing that Leno collects cars]. And about a week later I got a phone call from him and we chatted. It was fun to talk to Jay Leno. But he wasn't interested. That took a bit of wind out of my sails. It would have been huge. It would have made all the difference in the world.

We did the campaign for sixty days, and for about the first thirty days I held hope it would be "discovered." About two or three weeks before it expired, I was pretty well discouraged. I contacted directly for support all the members of the local DeLorean owners club, as well as those all across the globe, and in fact most of the money pledged came from owners.

Early in the campaign, you got a comment from a user with some advice about tweaking your video and the rewards levels, that maybe $35 for a DVD was too high. Were those a problem?

Werner: I don't think so. I've seen other projects that have had minimal rewards and done well. I really believe it's all about getting there with momentum ready to roll at the time you launch.

Acapelladiva's Opera Debut Phoenix CD Album
Kickstarter goal: $20,000
Raised: $6,595

Acapelladiva: Aurora Arias CD
Kickstarter goal: $3,000
Raised: $4,005

Julie Brown has a strong, soaring voice and a background in classic opera, giving her a unique place in the rich music scene of Austin, Texas. In September 2011, after years performing locally and giving voice lessons, she decided to go for it and try to record her own CD. She pulled together a creative Kickstarter campaign, with rewards that included copies of her music, a private concert, and the "Texas cowgirl outfit" she wore for a performance at the Texas state capitol. Her campaign fell short. Then she regrouped, tried again, and succeeded.

What did you learn from the first campaign that you fixed the second time?

Brown: I'd gotten so excited, wanting to do it really big. I wanted to sing with an orchestra. I researched it and, to hire the smallest orchestra, the cost was anywhere from $20,000 to $200,000. The second time I downscaled it. I thought, *the thing that's important is my voice.* So I downscaled it to just piano and voice. It's not a huge thing, not thousands and thousands of CDs. I'm probably gonna make 500 copies. It's a marketing tool, to at least get my voice out there. Now I plan to get out and do more live performances.

So, it was that simple. It's still worth doing, even scaled down?

Brown: It's really easy for artists to think, *I didn't make it, I'm gonna give up.* But just rethink it. Do it on a smaller scale. You can be successful.

Nectar and Elixir – bike seat clamp / bottle openers
March 2011
Kickstarter goal: $15,000
Raised: $1,291

Nectar and Elixir – seat clamp / bottle openers
April 2011
Kickstarter goal: $2,500
Raised: $4,403

The partners at Swarm, a design firm in Park City, Utah, had to try twice to find the winning Kickstarter formula for their innovative bicycle-seat clamps that function as handy-dandy bottle openers. After their first try crashed, falling way short of attracting $15,000, they tried again just weeks later, asking for a mere $2,500. In the "About

This Project" text for the second try, they began "Hey Kickstarters! Thanks for stopping by and checking out round 2 of our Nectar and Elixir project. We've done some serious renegotiation, and dropped our goal by over 80%. This time you can be sure that Project Seat Clamp is go for launch!" They also shot an entirely new video, containing more cycling action and a preamble explaining what they were calling their "relaunch": "Turns out that our previous goal was a little bit too steep . . . but the great thing about Kickstarter is, through the whole process, we've actually made some great contacts. We've met some domestic manufacturers, we met some distribution guys . . . these guys were able to work with us more, and we're able to work with a much lower goal."

The result: asking for much less, they got much more. They raised $4,403 the second time around. And by mid-2011, they had the cool clamps manufactured and shipped to thirsty cyclists worldwide.

What do you think went wrong the first time?

Garrett: The product was very niche. We were aware of that from the outset. We did feel like we'd get a little bit better response than we did in the first round, but what we learned was that just to be on Kickstarter was not nearly enough. It gets lost. Kickstarter had so many products, and now it has even more. Even then, we were getting lost. We were a smaller product without a whole lot of reach. On the first try we just weren't well connected.

On the second try we were able to use all the connections we made with the first attempt. So we connected with those people again. Most of those people rolled over; about 80 percent repledged. At that point we needed to double that number from new people. We kept a list of people who were doing Kickstarter updates on blogs, any Web portal that was reposting. Anything.

In lowering your fund-raising target, how much did you have to scale back your goals?

Garrett: We just lost a lot more money! The plan was to get the Kickstarter campaign to pay for tooling. And in that sense it worked. So we were just trying to reach a certain amount of money to pay for tooling so we could take the product from that point to whatever sales channels we planned to go into. And what we learned is that we were never going to be able to produce this product at a competitive rate unless we sold it direct. Then we still were not going to be able to make any money, so we killed it.

We realized from the outset that it's just a cool product, and we didn't expect it to sell huge numbers. We were hoping we would get more buy-in than we did, but we look at it as a promotion for our business, which is product design. And it worked. We had a lot of people contact us because of Kickstarter. We picked up at least two projects.

So, for you, Kickstarter was about free marketing more than this particular product?

Garrett: Yeah, it's an inexpensive way to get a lot of people to look at our products and our design company. Our company has been in existence for eight months. We formed the company and then saw that it's difficult to get the word out unless you have a big database, which we didn't. So we thought: *what's the best way to enter the market?* And that is to get products onto the market. Have people come to our website and learn more about the company.

In a way, it kind of kick-started your company . . .

Garrett: That's the way we look at it.

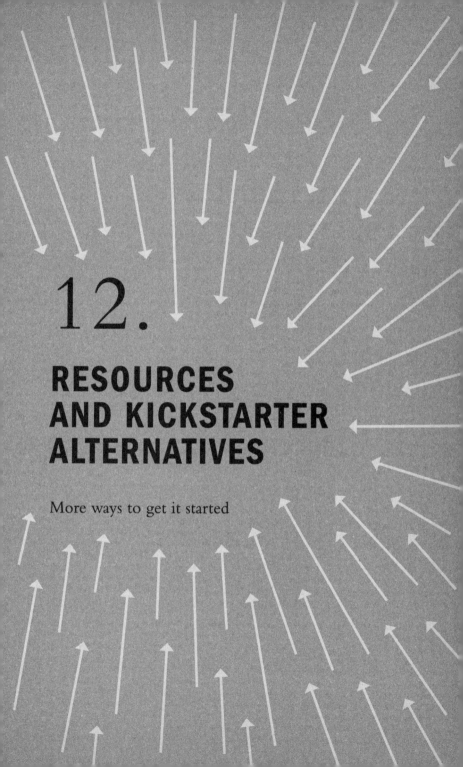

12.

RESOURCES AND KICKSTARTER ALTERNATIVES

More ways to get it started

KICKSTARTER ISN'T THE ONLY crowdfunding site on the Internet and certainly not the single resource that can help artists, entrepreneurs, and inventors who seek funding. Kickstarter's success, of course, has spawned imitation, homage, and general riffing on the concept. Several direct alternatives exist on the Web. Some approach project fund-raising differently. Others can supplement a Kickstarter campaign, such as facilities that offer assistance with rapid prototyping of a product concept or organizations that can help you work through the details of becoming a nonprofit. Some are aimed at businesses looking to get started. Others are more specifically for musicians or filmmakers.

If you're shopping around, here is a selection of the many diverse sites along with ideas that will get you thinking. For the latest links and news about various resources, follow @crowdfunding on Twitter (unaffiliated with this book or with Kickstarter).

For more information about any of the sites listed below—none are affiliated with this book—go to the URLs provided and read the FAQ or About pages. This list is representative and not an endorsement of any particular sites. Keep in mind that the Web is constantly changing. Sites come and go, and their missions may evolve.

A Little Like Kickstarter

ArtSpire

artspire.org

Artists must apply to this program of the New York Foundation for the Arts, which offers its "fiscally sponsored" artists a way to affiliate with 501(c)(3) tax-exempt organizations. Doing so allows artists to accept tax-deductible contributions and apply for grants that are usually restricted to nonprofits.

Crowdtilt

crowdtilt.com

They call what happens here group-funding rather than crowdfunding. In crowdfunding, many people fund an individual's project; in group-funding, a group pools money to fund an objective that benefits the entire group. Unlike Kickstarter, Crowdtilt can be used to throw a party or help someone with medical bills.

Feed the Muse

feedthemuse.net

A sort of Kickstarter clone, dominated by music projects, that doesn't have all-or-nothing funding thresholds.

IndieGoGo

indiegogo.com

IndieGoGo is a lot like Kickstarter; some have even called it a clone. The biggest difference is that, in seeking funds, you're not forced into an all-or-nothing system. If you're out to get $10,000 and you get $8,500, you can keep the $8,500. The company started in 2008 with a fixed funding model (all-or-nothing, like Kickstarter) but then moved away from it; it now offers both fixed funding and flexible funding. The fixed funding option has been used by many IndieGoGo project creators who need a minimum amount of money to follow through with their projects. As in Kickstarter, the deadline and threshold add a sense of urgency that you lose going the flexible funding route. According to IndieGoGo, flexible funding is ideal for projects that you can break into smaller goals or for which you have other funding sources.

RocketHub
rockethub.com

RocketHub matches "creatives" with "fuelers." They don't have thirteen creative categories, as Kickstarter does, but they do have tags that can be assigned to projects, like "freaky" or "nostalgia" or "sexy." It, too, is an all-or-nothing funding system, but RocketHub takes pledged money right away, via credit card or PayPal, instead of waiting until the end of a successful campaign. If a campaign doesn't meet its goal, pledge money is put into a pledger's RocketHub account. From there, the pledger can get the cash back, but many choose to use it to fund other projects.

USA Projects
usaprojects.org

A nonprofit that "connects people with great artists and helps them to make tax-deductible contributions to projects in the performing, visual, media, and literary arts." Before being accepted, an artist must have the blessing of "one of [the site's] partners or recognized organizations," which include hundreds of foundations, corporations, and arts organizations across the United States.

Not-for-Profit-y
CrowdRise
crowdrise.com

Crowdrise is for charitable causes and volunteer efforts, two types of fund-raising activities that are explicitly excluded from Kickstarter.

You can raise money by receiving pledges to run in a marathon, volunteer on weekends, or anything else that might inspire donations. Money goes to a charity you choose. The charities on CrowdRise are U.S.-based, 501(c)(3) nonprofits.

Fractured Atlas

fracturedatlas.org

Fractured Atlas is a nonprofit that offers a range of services to starving-artist types. Services include access to funding and health insurance. The site lists many film, dance, theater, visual arts, and other projects, and donors can make a tax-deductible contribution to Fractured Atlas earmarked for a particular effort. Members pay $95 a year.

Fundly

fundly.com

Fundly is a fund-raising platform for nonprofits, do-gooders, and others in need. It has funded projects by big organizations like Habitat for Humanity, Boys and Girls Clubs, and Teach for America but also by individuals to raise money for trips, to help with postdisaster recovery, and to defray costs during health crises. Also included are religious groups and political campaigns. Meg Whitman used Fundly to raise $20 million for her 2010 campaign for California governor.

Start Some Good

startsomegood.com

SSG is for social-change initiatives, "empowering people from around the world to become social innovators." Site organizers don't limit it to tax-deductible charities. The categories include "citizenship," "human rights," and "environment." A recent example: the "Cost of Freedom Voter ID App," designed to "cut through the confusion and quickly provide citizens with information on how to apply for a photo ID which they must show in order to vote."

YouHelp
youhelp.at

Available only in German-speaking countries but with plans to spread, this Austrian start-up is applying the crowdfunding model to nongovernmental organizations that offer international assistance.

More Music-y
ArtistShare

artistshare.com

ArtistShare calls itself a fan-funding site. Since 2003 it has allowed "fans to show appreciation for their favorite artists by funding their projects in exchange for access to the creative process." That means access to recording sessions, limited-edition recordings, and acknowledgment in liner notes. It's not an open platform for all musicians, however. You need to apply and be accepted.

Hifidelics
hifidelics.com

Hifidelics lets musicians raise money to create limited-edition releases (500 copies maximum) of albums on vinyl. If a project gets enough funding, the company will make the LP and sell it. There are no fees to use Hifidelics. If a project is successful, the musicians get 60 percent of all sales after production costs are covered.

PledgeMusic
pledgemusic.com

PledgeMusic is a Kickstarter-ish site just for music. It helps artists and bands "design a specifically tailored fund-raising campaign to raise money for their next release." As in Kickstarter, funds seekers invent rewards for donors, "anything from DJ-ing at your house party to attending a rehearsal, or even a movie and dinner with the band." It's also an all-or-nothing system.

Sellaband
sellaband.com

Sellaband is a European site where musicians can raise money to record music and go on tour. It is denominated in euros, but there are musicians from all over the world using it, including some from the United States.

Sites including **Bandcamp** (bandcamp.com) and **TuneCore** (tunecore.com) offer indie artists digital distribution of their music. In addition, **ReverbNation** (reverbnation.com) can help in getting gigs.

More Film-y
Slated
slated.com

Slated is a sort of high-end dating service for filmmakers and investors. It's not made for soliciting $50 donations. The site lists feature films (budgets $500,000–$15+ million) and documentaries with broad commercial appeal (budgets $250,000–$2 million). It's an exclusive site: anyone who applies to use it needs to be approved by two other members of the Slated community before the person's profile will be published. Investors are allowed to freely contact filmmakers, but not the other way around.

VODO
vodo.net

VODO has been described as Netflix-meets-Kickstarter for indie films. It's a peer-to-peer distribution platform for completed films (they don't store the films; you download using torrents). Users can download movies for free, and filmmakers can raise money by offering goodies around the movies in exchange for donations, like companion books, audio soundtracks. The Yes Men offered props from their film and raised $26,000.

Offbeatr
offbeatr.com
It was bound to happen. This start-up is trying to be a Kickstarter for makers of porno films.

Of course, seasoned filmmakers are accustomed to applying for grants, and there are plenty of them out there, places like **Cinereach** (cinereach.org/grants), **Rooftop Films** (rooftopfilms.com/info/produce_filmfundguidelines_shorts), and the **Sundance Institute** (sundance.org/programs/documentary-fund).

More Design-y

The "maker" revolution isn't so much about fund-raising as the idea that, if you have a design or product idea, you can prototype it yourself to see what it looks and feels like, and whether it really works. Facilities called "fabrication studios" and "maker cooperatives" and "hacker spaces" continue to sprout in many cities, providing training and access to equipment including computers, 3-D printers and high-tech industrial machinery for working with electronics, metal, plastic, wood, and textiles. These facilities often require you to join as a member and take lessons so that you can safely and productively use the equipment. TechShops have "dream consultants" on staff to guide you to the right equipment. Using a facility like this can be the precursor to taking a product or art design project to a crowdfunding resource like Kickstarter, where it always pays to have a prototype to show potential backers.

Check into the expanding list of locations for **TechShop** (techshop.ws) and **FabLabs** (fab.cba.mit.edu/about/labs/). There's also **NYC Resistor** (nycresistor.com) in Brooklyn, **NextFab Studio** (nextfabstudio.com) in Philadelphia, and **Phoenix Asylum** (phoenixasylum.org) in Boulder, Colorado, among many others.

More Sport-y

Involved Fan

involvedfan.com

Rather than helping artists make art, this site is where fans can help athletes finance their training and travel to tournaments. Fans can get autographed goodies, newsletters, Skype calls, and lessons. Athletes receive 80 percent of the money that is pledged to them. The site handles athlete newsletters and shipping of autographed items.

More Publishing-y

Unbound

unbound.co.uk

Based in England and denominated in British pounds, Unbound is open to authors in the United States and other countries who want to finance the self-publishing of a book via crowdfunding. Monty Python alumnus Terry Jones used Unbound to finance a series of wacky books. The projects have predefined backer rewards packages (digital book, hardback, signed edition, goodie bag, launch party, lunch with author) at preset pledge amounts that simplify the task of thinking up prizes for backers.

Magcloud

magcloud.com

This isn't a crowdfunding site but a way to self-publish and sell magazines and other publications. You design your publication in a traditional print layout, with pages that readers turn, and then use the site to sell it in both digital and print versions. Magcloud, operated by a division of Hewlett Packard, will print and ship the paper versions of magazines to customers on demand.

Blurb (blurb.com), **CreateSpace** (createspace.com), **Lightning Source** (lightningsource.com), and **Lulu** (lulu.com) are among the best-known options for publishing a book on a print-on-demand basis.

More Photojournalism-y
Emphas.is
emphas.is

Yes, there's a crowdfunding site for photojournalism. On Emphas. is, photojournalists pitch projects directly to the public and offer rewards at different pledge levels. In 2012, the site also debuted Emphas.is Books to fund the creation of photography books.

More Arts-and-Crafts-y
Etsy
etsy.com

Not a crowdfunding site but rather a big online marketplace place where artisans can get funding for stuff they make by offering it for sale directly to consumers. It's like a giant crafts fair, with everything from handmade soaps and jewelry to a 500-gigabyte external hard drive in the casing of a Super Mario Bros Nintendo game cartridge. Items are often made on demand in response to orders, so, like Kickstarter, Etsy can minimize the need to build up a large inventory before the customers have arrived.

Overseas Options
Ulule
ulule.com

Ulule is an international site that has crowdfunded "creative, innovative, or community-minded projects" worldwide, from record albums to humanitarian missions.

New Jelly
newjelly.com

This European crowdfunding site has many of the same rules as Kickstarter; denominated in euros.

More Business-y

In business, financial backers generally are looking for a piece of the action and a return on their investment. They give funds to a company as either equity or debt—an ownership piece of the company or a loan that must be repaid. Kickstarter doesn't work that way—you never sell any equity on your project, and you don't take on any debt from your backers. In fact, for decades it was illegal in the United States for a company to seek equity investment via crowdfunding from anyone but "accredited investors," which means rich people with a net worth of at least $1 million. That law was put into place in 1933 as a way to protect regular people from scams and overly risky bets. But critics said it locked start-up companies out of a way to raise capital, and it locked small investors out of a chance to get in early on breakout investments that have a lot of financial upside (along with a lot of risk). In April 2012, President Barack Obama signed the Entrepreneur Access to Capital Act, part of the bigger JOBS Act (the acronym for Jumpstart Our Business Startups), which was designed to let companies raise as much as $1 million per year from anyone, without having to do a public offering. As the Economist explained: "For the first time ordinary investors would be allowed to put up to $10,000 in small businesses that are not registered with the Securities and Exchange Commission, enabling Joe Schmo to win big if the company becomes the next Google." Online portals for equity crowdfunding are expected to spring up, but exactly how the system will be implemented, circa mid-2012, remained in the hands of government regulators. Keep an eye on developments.

Certainly, some people who are running cool projects on Kickstarter are in fact starting companies. And they may be working separately with more traditional angel and seed investors at the same time, or soon after their Kickstarter campaigns.

Meanwhile, a variety of sites can help match business ideas with possible funding. Here are some worth knowing about.

Angel List

angel.co

Angel List is a sort of social network for serious business startups and serious investors. Angel investors who have made multiple $25,000-plus angel investments are welcome. Startups create a profile that can be seen by investors, and they can "follow" investors. It's supposed to be a great way to get a pitch in front of a lot of rich people at once.

AppsFunder

appsfunder.com

AppsFunder is a Kickstarter-style site for Apple and Android app creators. You list an app and offer various rewards for different pledge amounts. Backers can get a cheap per-sales copy of the app but—here's the twist—they can pledge large sums and receive a cash slice of your earnings once your app is published on AndroidMarket or in the Apple Appstore. It's typical to offer $75 in revenue sharing for a $25 pledge.

Quirky

quirky.com

They call Quirky a "social product development" site. It's given birth to slick products you can now buy, like the Broom Groomer (a dustpan with plastic teeth that can extract the junk stuck in a broom) and Thor (extensible windshield ice scraper with an X-shaped blade). The ideas come from regular people. "It's time that we make invention accessible. It's time that we invent together," says Quirky's manifesto. "A product at Quirky isn't born in the boardroom. It's born in the living room. It's born on the drive home. It's bred by people from all walks of life. People just like you."

Product ideas that are submitted are voted on and refined with ideas from the site's users, and the Quirky team helps design, spec, and prototype select products. Products that get enough presales are then produced and sold. The original inventors as well as anyone who had any input into the process gets reimbursed. "We track down to a fraction of a percentage how much input each community member had over the successful development of a product. Every time one unit of a product sells, all the people involved get paid," they explain. Like Kickstarter, it's also a place to buy unique gifts.

Accelerators, Boot Camps, and Incubators

Start-up companies have options beyond crowdfunding, including the many organizations that regional groups have organized to foster economic development and those that hungry investors have established to get a piece of the next Facebook.

Many boot camps and incubators are founded by angel investors who nurture and mentor fledgling companies—in exchange for a piece of ownership, often 10 percent of the company. The startups selected for entry into the programs receive a small amount of funding, often $20,000 or less. They move into the offices of the boot camp or incubator for a certain period, whether weeks or months, honing their products and ideas and preparing to pitch to investors. At the end, they usually have a Demo Day, when they present to a large audience of investors. Here are some of these types of sources:

AlphaLab, Pittsburgh, PA (alphalab.org)

Bootup Labs, Vancouver, BC (bootuplabs.com)

Capital Factory, Austin, TX (capitalfactory.com)

DreamIt Ventures, Philadelphia, PA (dreamitventures.com)

Good Company Ventures, Philadelphia, PA (goodcompanygroup .org)

Junto Partners, Salt Lake City, UT (juntopartners.com)

Seed Hatchery, Memphis, TN (seedhatchery.com)

TechStars, Boulder, CO (techstars.com)

Y-Combinator, Mountain View, CA (ycombinator.com)

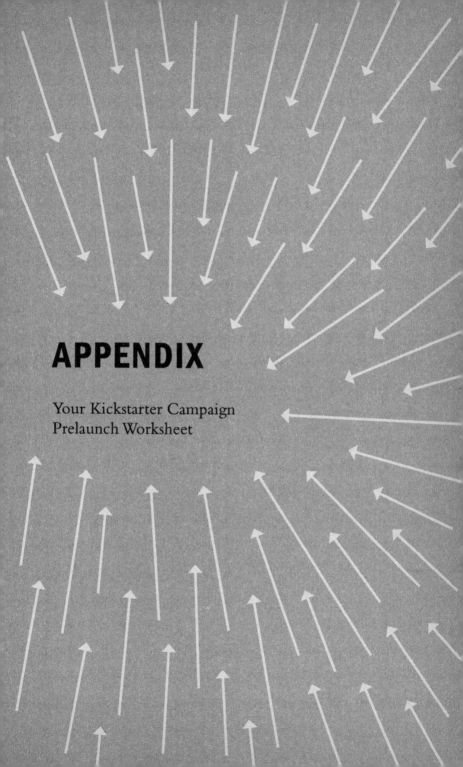

APPENDIX

Your Kickstarter Campaign
Prelaunch Worksheet

KICKSTARTER CAMPAIGNS are a lot of work, so you'll want to make a good plan well in advance of the launch date. This Prelaunch Worksheet asks important questions you'll need to answer before presenting your project to the world. Some of these answers will need to be input directly into Kickstarter.com. Others are simply useful for planning, organizing, and marketing your campaign. Let's go!

Thinking about Your Project

In as few words as possible, give your campaign an intriguing and descriptive title. If your product has a name, it can serve as the title of your campaign.

_____

_____

What makes your project unique and special? Does it give people new capabilities? Is it art that looks at the world in a new way? List three ways in which your project is original:

_____

_____

_____

_____

The first text people may see explaining your project is a 135-character description in the widget for the project at Kickstarter.com. That's about the length of the previous sentence. How would you describe your project to a friend or stranger in one sentence, in a way that makes it sound awesome, unique, and worthy of a significant pledge?

_____

_____

_____

_____

Think about your personal story and how it relates to your Kickstarter project. What elements of your own story might be intriguing to, say, a reporter or someone making a movie about your life and your Kickstarter project?

_____

_____

_____

The Basics

Do you meet the basic qualifications to undertake a Kickstarter campaign listed on page 25?

Does your project NOT involve any of the prohibited items and subject matter listed on page 26?

Is your project literally a "project," with a defined product (or creative production) that will emerge at the end? Can you state the goal in one sentence?

_____

_____

_____

Does your project have a "creative purpose" that fits into one of the following official Kickstarter categories:

→ Art   → Film   → Publishing
→ Comics   → Food   → Technology
→ Dance   → Games   → Theater
→ Design★   → Music
→ Fashion   → Photography

★Kickstarter has added requirements for product design and technology projects. Most likely to be approved for launch are projects for "products with strong aesthetics" and those for which a functional prototype can be demonstrated.

Researching the Field

Search Kickstarter.com for at least five previous projects from creators based in your city or local area. Name them here for future reference:

_____

_____

_____

_____

_____

Search Kickstarter.com for five previous projects whose category or product is similar to yours. Name them here for future reference:

_____

_____

_____

_____

_____

Time and Money

About how much money do you think you will need for your creative project? _____

Using the worksheets in chapter 2, how much will you need to raise on Kickstarter? _____

Using your own ideas and those provided in chapter 3, try to list rewards you can offer to backers. For starters, you can estimate how they'll match with different dollar-pledge levels here. The financial worksheets in chapter 2 can help you calculate more precisely what pledge amounts may make sense for different rewards.

→ $1	→ $35	→ $500
→ $5	→ $50	→ $1000
→ $10	→ $100	
→ $25	→ $250	

Is there a reason your campaign should run for longer or fewer than 30 days? Chapter 5 can help you determine an ideal duration. Indicate here how many days you'd like your campaign to run for:

_____

When your campaign launches, make a note of its end date and look at the calendar to see how weekends, holidays, and other factors may affect or interfere with your ability to draw pledges and attention during your campaign (i.e., gifting holidays like Mother's Day and Christmas can be useful if your project is a givable item):

CAMPAIGN END DATE: _____

INTERFERING EVENTS: _____

Kickstarter Video Checklist

There's no secret recipe for making a successful Kickstarter video, but there are recommended ingredients. When you're done making your video, you should be able to check off the items on this list. (For much more advice, see chapter 6.)

The video

- → tells viewers what exactly your project is about within its first 20 to 30 seconds
- → has clear, professional-sounding audio
- → demonstrates a functional or advanced prototype of your product (for products) or an impressive example of your talent (for art/performance projects)
- → shows the project creator (you) as passionate about the project and completely capable of making it work
- → contains text at the end stating that it's a Kickstarter project, including the URL for your Kickstarter page

Scoping Out Backers

Lining up backers: You don't have to share this list with anyone, but start thinking about the people you might be able to rely on for pledges, including your family, friends, and fans. You'll want to get in touch with these people *before* your campaign launch.

Possible "big kahunas" who may give large pledges:

_____

_____

_____

_____

_____

_____

_____

_____

_____

_____

Other people or organizations to contact:

_____

_____

_____

_____

_____

_____

_____

_____

_____

_____

_____

_____

_____

_____

Media Planning

Getting attention via the mass media can be crucial to a successful Kickstarter campaign. You'll want to have an ample list of media contacts prepared before you kick off your campaign, and you'll want to be ready to make contacts as soon as you launch, using the advice offered in chapter 8. After you reach out to your media contacts, it's important to be organized, gathering phone numbers and e-mail addresses, logging your contact history, and noting how you need to follow up. Contact sheets like the ones that follow can be helpful.

Local Media

It's important to let local media know about your project. Local coverage can lead to broader national coverage. It also builds your credibility for potential backers and helps you tell your story. In any city, there are plenty of local media outlets to choose from: TV stations, radio stations, daily newspapers, weekly alternative papers, town gazettes and pennysavers, local blogs, etc. Use a contact sheet like the one below to list local media targets and as much as you can learn about how to contact the appropriate people who work for them. Refer to your list above of other Kickstarter projects from your area—research the outlets they received their media coverage and which reporters filed the story.

Media outlet			
Have they covered Kickstarter projects?			
How?			
Possible contact person			
Contact information (phone / e-mail)			
Contact made?			
Result / next steps			

National/Global and Special Interest Media

Before you launch, you'll want to identify websites and blogs that cover the topic your project fits into. Are you working on a revolutionary type of bicycle handlebar? Build a big list of cycling blogs and ways to contact them. Refer to your list above of other Kickstarter projects similar to yours and note which blogs and other special-interest media outlets covered them.

Social Media

Media outlet			
Have they covered Kickstarter projects?			
How?			
Possible contact person			
Contact information (phone / e-mail)			
Contact made?			
Result / next steps			

It will make sense for you to set up social media accounts for your Kickstarter campaign that are separate from your personal accounts, though you may also want to contact your existing online friends and followers. It may also make sense to establish a website for your project, if you don't already have one. Indicate which online accounts you set up for your campaign and how people can reach them.

Facebook URL: _____

Twitter ID: _____

Website URL: _____

YouTube Channel URL: _____

Other Influencers

Call them connectors, mavens, whatever. We all know a few people who seem to know everyone and are great at getting the word out. List some people you know who might be able to spread the news about your Kickstarter campaign. Then don't be shy about letting these human hubs know what's happening.

_____

_____

_____

_____

_____

_____

_____

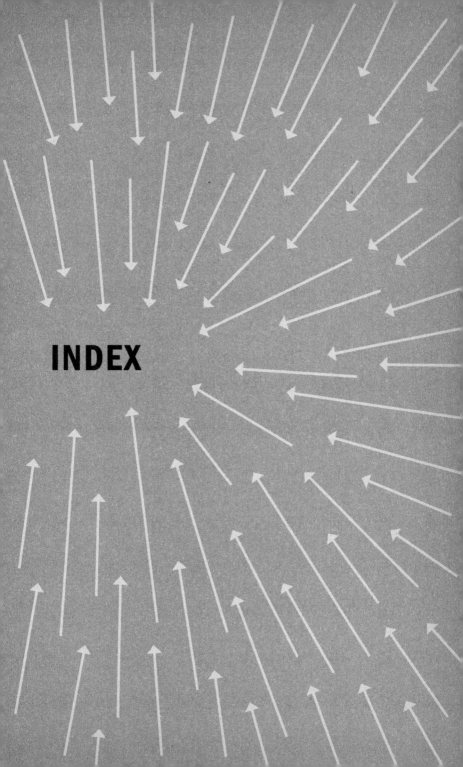

INDEX

Headings in **boldface** denote names of projects.

Acapelladiva, 189–90
accelerators, 206
addresses, 25, 175
adjustments, 113
Adler, Charles, 13
advertising, 45, 125
Allison Weiss makes a full-length record! 115–16
AlphaLab, 206
Amazon Payments, 25, 41, 44, 45, 109–10, 164
The American Revolution *See* Lichtenstein, Bill
amultiverse.com, 77
Angel List, 205
approval, 107
AppsFunder, 205
art and artists, 14, 27
  crowdfunding, 196–98, 203
  finances, 35–41
  Joshua Harker, 16–17, 89, 123–24, 165–67
  sample rewards, 60–61
  Tell Em Steve Dave, 64–65
  See also Detroit Needs A Statue of Robocop!
ArtistShare, 199
Artspire, 196
Atijas, Rafael, 58
audience, 129–31, 142, 154–55, 184

backer reports, 113
backers, 18, 73–80
  breaking down costs for, 47–49
  convincing, 22
  Matt Haughey, 64, 80–83, 128, 149
  prelaunch worksheet, 214
  unhappy, 174
  updates for, 57
  See also friends and family; rewards
Backhausdance is Performing in New York at Joyce SoHo, 63
Bandcamp, 200
bank account, 25, 109–10
Berlinger, Yehuda, 65
Betabeat, 23
big kahunas, 78–83, 156
biography, 109
blogs and blogging, 81, 83, 121, 138–45
  Betabeat, 23
  Boing Boing, 77, 130

Colossal, 130
Futuregirl, 130
Swissmiss, 121, 138–40
TechCrunch, 141–43
updates, 191
Blurb, 202
Boing Boing, 77, 130
books *See* publishing
boot camps, 206
Bootup Labs, 206
Brown, Julie, 189–90
bulk orders, 39
Burlew, Rich, 29, 63, 67
business people, 74, 158
business start-ups
  beyond Kickstarter, 36, 43, 59, 192
  crowdfunding, 204, 206
  not Kickstarter mission, 27
  public relations, 143

campaign page, 30, 107–11, 182
campaigns, 18
  categories, 13, 27, 108
  final days, 149–60
  followup, 153–54
  grinding through, 117–18
  lessons in failure, 181–92
  one-time performance/arts, 35–41
  product-oriented, 41–43
  timing of, 151, 160
  worksheets, 35–43
Capital Factory, 206
charities *See* nonprofit organizations
Chen, Perry, 12–14, 184
Chenell, Dave, 23, 182
Cinereach, 201
Cleckner, Eric, 23, 182
Coffee Joulies, 28
cold calls, 74, 135, 144, 158
Coldewey, Devin, 141–43
collaborations, 55
Colossal, 130
comebacks, 149–60
comedy festival *See* theater
comics, 27
  Rich Burlew, 29, 63, 67
  personalized rewards, 63
  Jonathan Rosenberg, 77
  sample rewards, 60–61
comments, 113, 116–17, 158
contact information, 109
contact list, 122
copyright, 103–104
costs, 35, 37–41, 44
Crain, Zach
  duration, 89

fulfillment, 175
funding progress, 118
fund-raising goal, 45–46
rewards, 58, 62, 69
video, 101–103
Crania Anatomica Filigre, 89, 123–24, 165–67
CreateSpace, 202
creative categories, 13, 27, 108
creative experiences *See* rewards
creative purpose, 27
creators, 18, 28
credit cards, 25, 75, 175, 183–87
criteria for project, 25
Cross, David, 13
crowdfunding, 15, 73, 83, 195–206
CrowdRise, 197–99
crowdsourcing, 15, 80
Crowdtilt, 196
Currier, Micah, 47
customer service, 166

dance, 27, 60–61, 63, 198
dashboard, 76–77, 112–13
deadlines, 13–14, 30, 163
debit cards, 25
debt, 14
Dennis, Felix, 22
design and designers, 9–11, 14
  Rafael Atijas, 58
  crowdfunding, 201, 205–206
  Micah Currier, 47
  Tina Roth Eisenberg, 138–40
  Taylor Levy, 97–98, 121, 172–75
  Russell Maret, 47
  rewards, 60–62
  David Sosnow, 176–77
  Swarm, 54, 130, 169–70, 182, 190–92
  Scott Thrift, 9–11, 16, 74, 75, 121–22, 170–71
  user-interface, 13
  Chei-Wei Wang, 97–98, 121, 172–75
  Scott Wilson, 14, 29, 58
  See also Crain, Zach; Hartung, Josh
Detroit Needs A Statue of Robocop! 21, 23, 46, 75–76, 78–79, 116–18
disaster recovery, 198
domain name, 38
donors *See* backers
Double Fine Adventure, 28–29
Dreaming in Stainless, 188–89
DreamIt Ventures, 206
Drumm, Brook, 57–58
duration, 30, 87–89, 108, 212

e20: System Evolved, 65–66
eBay, 15, 23
effort, 22–24
Eisenberg, Tina Roth, 138–40
Elevation Dock, 82, 88,
 100–101
e-mail
 backers, 74, 113, 114
 bloggers, 139–40, 141
 cold, 130, 135
 final push, 158
 media, 144, 155
 post campaign, 164
Emphas.is, 203
endorsements, 159, 195
entrepreneurs, 80–83, 128,
 142, 204
environment, 198
equipment, 38–39
equity, 14
Etsy, 140, 203
events, 131, 135–36, 143
experiences, creative *See* rewards

FabLabs, 201
Facebook
 for backers, 74
 final push, 159
 media publicity, 123, 155
 project page, 69, 110, 117,
  125–26, 186
 referring source, 77
 shared interest, 158
 video sharing, 103
failure, 181–92
family *See* friends and family
fans
 crowdfunding, 202
 of endorsers, 159
 existing bases, 28, 67, 77,
  82, 83
 funding sites, 199
 outsiders, 75
fan sites, 123
fashion, 27, 60–61
favorites, Kickstarter, 22, 113,
 136–37, 158
feedback, 110
Feed the Muse, 196
fees, 41, 44, 45, 110, 164
festivals *See* theater
film and filmmakers, 15, 27, 29
 crowdfunding, 198, 200–201
 finances, 35–41
 Jennifer Fox, 44, 94
 Aurora Guerrero, 23, 24, 129,
  153–56
 Nathaniel Hansen, 65, 128–29

Jacob Krupnick, 112–13,
 167–68
Lucas McNelly, 44–45, 68–69,
 73–74, 79–80, 116, 149–52
sample rewards, 60–61
Chris Schlarb, 115
**A Sustainable Reality:
 Redefining Roots**, 136
Craig Werner, 188–89
See also Lichtenstein, Bill
financial worksheets, 17, 44–47
follow-ups, 135
food, 27, 60–61
 See also Taylor, Pete
forums, 66, 131
Fox, Jennifer, 44, 94
Fractured Atlas, 198
Freaker USA *See* Crain, Zach
Frequently Asked Questions, 57,
 111, 116–17
friends and family, 22, 73–74,
 157–58, 186–87
FTL: Faster Than Light, 28–29
fulfillment, 163–77
funding models, 14, 33–34,
 196–97, 199
funding progress, 88, 112, 123,
 150, 153, 157
Fundly, 198
fund-raisers, outside, 136
fund-raising goals
 and failure, 185, 192
 setting, 13–14, 23, 33–47
 worksheet, 212
Futuregirl, 130

games and game developers,
 23, 27
 Yehuda Berlinger, 65
 Dave Chenell, 23, 182
 Eric Cleckner, 23, 182
 Double Fine Adventure,
  28–29
 FTL: Faster Than Light,
  48–49
 inXile Entertainment, 66
 sample rewards, 60–61
 Gary Sarli, 65–66
 Daniel Solis, 66–67
Garrett, Wesley, 130, 169–70,
 190–92
Gerhardt, Dan, 174
Girl Walk // All Day, 112–13,
 167–68
Glif, 14, 174
**Goats Book IV: Inhuman
 Resources**, 77
Good Company Ventures, 206
Google, 11, 111, 126, 131, 144, 164

graFighters, 23, 182
great white whales, 78–83, 156
**Gremolata & Cancellaresca
 Milanese**, 47
Groupon, 69
Guerrero, Aurora, 23, 24, 129,
 153–56
guidelines, 108

Hansen, Nathaniel, 65, 128–29
Harker, Joshua, 16–17, 89,
 123–24, 165–67
Hartung, Josh, 16, 41–43, 125,
 130, 136–37, 176–77
hate mail, 82
Haughey, Matt, 64, 80–83, 128,
 149
health crises, 198
Hifidelics, 199
Hopkins, Casey, 82, 88, 100–101
Hotelet, Pete, 78–79
human rights, 198
The HuMn Wallet, 127

incentives *See* rewards
incubators, 206
IndieGoGo, 196–97
international assistance, 199
inventory, 35, 36, 43, 166, 177
investment, 14, 204
Involved Fan, 202
inXile Entertainment, 66

**Jekyll and Hyde: The Music
 Video**, 135–36
Jenna Communications, 143–45
Junto Partners, 206

karma, 69
Keep Music Indie, 115
Kickstarter
 statistics, 181
Kickstarter School, 108
Kiva, 15
Krakauskas, Lauren, 102
Krochet Kids Peru, 62
Krupnick, Jacob, 112–13, 167–68

launch, 107, 110–11
legal issues, 172–75
Leno, Jay, 188
Levy, Taylor, 97–98, 121, 172–75
Lichtenstein, Bill
 backers, 74–75, 78
 build the buzz, 122
 campaign grind, 23–24
 duration, 89
 feedback, 117
 frantic finish, 159–60

fund-raising goal, 44
rewards, 69
video, 94
Lightning Source, 202
LinkedIn, 123, 126
loans, 15, 204
local appeal, 75–76
Londer, Abbey
backers, 75, 79
building buzz, 123, 124, 137
duration, 88
updates, 114–15
video, 98–99
Loog Guitar, 58
Loomi See Hartung, Josh
love notes, 175
LucasArts, 29
Lulu, 202
LunaTik, 14, 29, 58

magazines See newspapers/
magazines
Magcloud, 202
manufacturing, 29, 166, 173
Maret, Russell, 47
markets and marketing, 74,
129–31, 171, 203
McNelly, Lucas, 44–45, 68–69,
73–74, 79–80, 116, 149–52
media, 74, 127–31, 187, 215–18
See also online media; print
media
media plans, 122–24
Mellan, Oliver, 102
mementos, 55
MetaFilter, 80
momentum, 154, 156, 158,
188–89
Mosquita Y Mari, 23, 24, 129,
153–56
movies See film and filmmakers
music and musicians, 12–13,
16, 27, 29
Julie Brown, 189–90
crowdfunding, 196, 199–200
finances, 35–41
rewards, 60–61, 62
April Smith, 115
Theoretics, 135–36
Alison Weiss, 115–16, 125
Nano Whitman, 11, 62, 93,
95–96
Peter Wolf, 78
My Reincarnation, 94

Nectar and Elixir, 54, 130,
169–70, 182, 190–92
networking, 74, 82, 154–55
New Jelly, 203

newsletters, 113, 202
newspapers/magazines, 115,
130–31, 144, 155, 159, 184
NextFab Studio, 201
niche markets, 142, 191
nongovernmental organizations,
199
nonprofit organizations, 27,
63–64, 195, 197–99
NYC Resistor, 201

Offbeatr, 201
one-time performance/arts
projects
campaigns, 35–41
online media, 11–12, 124–27,
132–33
See also blogs and blogging;
social media
online storage, 12, 40
online stores, 38
**The Order of the Stick Reprint
Drive**, 29, 63, 67
ownership, 14, 204

parties, 39, 135
passion, 30, 65, 93, 139
patronage, 16
Pebble project, 68
peer-to-peer distribution, 200
Pen Type-A, 97–98, 121, 138,
172–75
Phoenix Asylum, 201
photography, 27, 60–61, 203
photo-sharing sites, 126
piracy, 12
pitch, 108–109
PledgeMusic, 199
pledge revenue, 39–41
pledges, 13–14, 17, 18, 30, 35
contingent, 78
international, 39, 43, 64
levels and rewards, 64–67
one-time performance/arts
projects, 37
tax deductible? 63–64
pledge trends, 56–57
podcasts, 183–87
political campaigns, 198
pornography, 12, 201
postcards, 166
premieres, 167–68
presales, 58, 205–206
The Present, 9–11, 16, 74, 75,
121–22, 170–71
press See print media
preview link, 107, 110
print media, 113, 115–16,
121–22, 143–44, 155

See also newspapers/
magazines
Printrbot, 57–58
procrastination, 87
product design See design, and
designers
product development, 16
product-oriented campaign, 41–43
profit-and-loss-statements See
financial worksheets
prohibitions, 25–26, 55
project categories See creative
categories
projects
bundling, 66
definition, 27–28
Project of the Day, 22, 136–37
proposal, 107
prototypes
challenges, 173
crowdfunding, 201, 205
crowdsourcing, 195
functional, 29, 82–83, 103
Provost, Tom, 174
public awareness, 79–80
publicity stunts, 33, 134
public relations, 11, 127–28,
143–45
publishing, 27
crowdfunding, 202
Felix Dennis, 22
graphic novels, 15
rewards, 60–61, 62
Web comics, 21

quality control, 166
**A Question of Ethics Podcast
Series**, 183–87
Quirky, 205–206

radio, 160, 183, 187
receipts, forecasting, 35
referring sources, 77
regulations See requirements
religious groups, 198
requirements, 13–14, 25, 108
research, 38, 64, 211–12
ReverbNation, 200
rewards, 18, 55–61
$1, 68–69
campaign page, 108
costs, 35, 39–41, 44
delivering, 163–77
and failure, 185
limited availability, 57, 68, 111,
113, 165–66
matching to pledge levels,
64–67
one-time performance/arts

projects, 37
personalized, 40, 55, 62–63, 67–68, 135–36, 185
pretesting, 66–67
prohibited, 26, 55
strategies, 53–54
tweaking, 67–68, 189–90
RIOT *See* Londer, Abbey
Robocop See Detroit Needs A Statue of Robocop!
RocketHub, 197
Romo - The Smartphone Robot, 29, 46, 59
Rooftop Films, 201
Rosenberg, Jonathan, 77
rules *See* requirements

sacrifice, 22
Sarli, Gary, 65–66
SAVORx *See* Taylor, Pete
Schafer, Tim, 28–29
Schlarb, Chris, 115
sculpture See art and artists
Seed Hatchery, 206
seed money, 27
Seid, Peter, 29, 46, 59
Sellaband, 200
shared interest, 129, 218
sharing, 12, 110
Sherlock, Jennifer, 143–45
shipping, 39–40, 43, 64, 164–67, 170, 177
site hosting, 38
Slated, 200
sleep strikes, 151–52
Smith, April, 115
social change, 198
social media
to build buzz, 124–27, 144
prelaunch worksheet, 218
YouTube, 11, 99, 126
social networks, 11, 113, 123
LinkedIn, 123, 126
See also Facebook; Twitter
Solis, Daniel, 66–67
Sosnow, David, 176–77
soundtracks, 104
spam, 114, 123, 157
sponsored links, 125
sponsors, 44–45
sports, 202
Staff Pick, 22, 136–37
Start Some Good, 198
story, 12–17, 108–109, 128–29, 145
street fairs, 176
Strickler, Yancey, 13, 28
success
psychology of, 149

rate of, 181
Sundance Film Festival, 15, 24, 201
surveys, 113, 164, 174, 175
A Sustainable Reality: Redefining Roots, 136
Swarm, 54, 130, 169–70, 182, 190–92
Swissmiss, 121, 138–40

target amount *See* fund-raising goals
tax deductions, 63–64, 198
Taylor, Pete
backers/rewards, 67–68, 74
campaign grind, 23, 117, 156–58
fund-raising, 48–49, 136, 158
publicity stunt, 134–35
TechCrunch, 141–43
technology, 27
crowdfunding, 205
Brook Drumm, 57–58
Dan Gerhardt, 174
Casey Hopkins, 82, 88, 100–101
The HuMn Wallet, 127
Tom Provost, 174
sample rewards, 60–61
Peter Seid, 29, 46, 59
TechShop, 201
TechStars, 206
television, 127, 134–35, 143
Tell Em Steve Dave, 64–65
terminology, Kickstarter, 17–18
theater, 13, 27, 35–41, 60–61, 198
See also Londer, Abbey
Theoretics, 135–36
threshold pledge system, 33–34
Thrift, Scott, 9–11, 16, 74, 75, 121–22, 170–71
TikTok+LunaTik, 14, 29, 58
time, value of, 65
timing, 151, 160
travel, 40
TuneCore, 200
tweak, 107, 110, 189
Twitter
@crowdfunding, 195
for backers, 74, 81, 83
campaign feed, 126
final push, 151–52
media publicity, 123
project page, 69, 110
referring source, 77
shared interest, 158

Ulule, 203
Unbound, 202

updates, 57, 113, 114–16, 163, 191
USA Projects, 197
Utara, 66–67

venture capital, 182
videos
and failure, 182, 185–86, 191
fixed cost, 38
Kickstarter, 93–104
prelaunch worksheet, 213
promotional, 139, 188
and the story, 108
viral, 115, 123–24
viral posts and videos, 115, 123–24, 130
VODO, 200
volume discounts, 39, 166
volunteer efforts, 197–98

Walley, Brandon See Detroit Needs A Statue of Robocop!
Wang, Chei-Wei, 97–98, 121, 172–75
Wasteland 2, 66
websites
free, 11–12
MakerCapitalist.com, 41
setting up, 38, 40, 43, 124–25
Weiss, Alison, 115–16, 125
Werner, Craig, 188–89
We Scream: Voices From The Ice Cream Underground, 115
white knights, 78–83, 156
Whitman, Nano, 11, 62, 93, 95–96
Wikipedia, 11, 15
Wilson, Scott, 14, 29, 58
word of mouth, 154
worksheets, 17, 35–43, 209–18
worst-case scenario, 66

Y-Combinator, 206
A Year Without Rent, 44–45, 68–69, 73–74, 116, 149–52
YouHelp, 199
YouTube, 11, 99, 126

Want More Tips on Crowdfunding Your Next Project?

Visit quirkbooks.com/ kickstarterhandbook to:

→ Read an interview with author Don Steinberg

→ Get more resources to help launch your project

→ Post about your Kickstarter story

→ Join the conversation